Limerick County Library

WITH~~~~~~~~~~~~~~~STOCK

30012 **00615303** 4

Wildlife Guide

Brazil

WITHDRAWN FROM STOCK

D1464969

NEW
HOLLAND

Limerick
County Library

918.1

Wildlife Guide

Brazil

John Malathronas

CONTENTS

INTRODUCTION

Brazil is rapidly becoming the ultimate eco-destination for green-minded travellers. With its large stretches of raw wilderness populated by unique flora and fauna, it is a place as fascinating and diverse as anyone can hope to find on our planet.

Apart from the numerous state parks, private reserves, ranches (*fazendas*) and ecological stations scattered throughout the country, there are currently 62 national parks in Brazil, making up 7% of its landmass. Their administration is decentralized and varies from state to state but, as a rule, they are under the jurisdiction of the Brazilian Environmental and Natural Renewable Resources Institute (IBAMA), an organization that is not as enthusiastic about mass tourism as is Embratur, the Brazilian State Tourism Authority. This accounts not only for the pristine environments of the national parks but also for the big variation in their services and accessibility: some are luxurious and well mapped (Iguaçu); some have no infrastructure (Jaú); some are closed to the public (Viruá); and others have a rigorous system of permits and visitor controls (Fernando de Noronha).

This book describes Brazil's many biomes and concentrates on representative national parks, focusing on their ability to showcase the wildlife of each region.

Top Spots to See Animals

Visitors flock to the Amazon in the hope of seeing its much-serenaded wildlife close-up; and yet the rainforest is a difficult place for the untrained eye to spot the well-camouflaged wildlife. The best places to see animals in Brazil are:

The Pantanal
Parque Nacional das Emas
Itatiaia (bird life)
Fernando de Noronha
(dolphins and sea turtles)

Opposite, top to bottom:
A jaguar crossing the river;
a motorboat with tourists speeds
across the river in Pantanal; a
white-knee tarantula.

Introduction

PLANNING YOUR TRIP

If you are organizing your trip yourself, remember that the distances between cities are enormous. Buses are cheap, safe and comfortable, but unless your time is unlimited, it is likely that you will need some flights to cover the ground. Flights within Brazil are not as expensive as they used to be with the advent of low-cost carriers like GOL, but an air pass is still something you may want to consider.

Note that outside the main tourist hot spots people will not speak anything other than Portuguese, so arm yourself with a phrase book and try to learn some basic tenets of the language. Some travellers believe that Spanish will help them get by – a wrong assumption. What they will discover is that they are occasionally understood, but, as the Brazilian accent is very different, they do not comprehend anything in return.

Nature operators

Brazil, untouched as it is by mass tourism, is uniquely suited for adventure activities. Its size and varied climate also ensure that there is something to do and somewhere to go year-round. The atmosphere of discovery and exploration is ever present, even in organized tours – not a bad idea if this is your first visit to the country. Most of the companies below will allow you to travel independently and join them locally, so where they operate from is irrelevant.

Brazil Adventures (www.brazil-adventures.com) is US-based, offers packages of eco-cultural adventures and can customize them to groups and individuals with special interests.

Journey Latin America (www.journeylatinamerica.co.uk) is the UK's foremost Latin American specialist offering trips or tailor-made excursions in all of Brazil's biomes.

Discovery Initiatives (www.discoveryinitiatives.co.uk) specializes in the Southern Pantanal area where its employees work with local *fazendas* (ranches) to provide tailor-made nature tours of the region.

What to Pack

• A wide-brimmed hat, sunglasses and a good sunscreen lotion.
• Shorts and swimming costume.
• At least one pair of long cotton trousers (or a light tracksuit).
• Short- and long-sleeved shirts.
• A mosquito net and insect repellent.
• A daypack.
• A good pair of hiking boots or sneakers with waterproof soles.
• A pair of black shoes – despite their laid-back attitude, Brazilians like to dress up at night.
• A rain poncho and a plastic bag to keep items such as cameras and binoculars dry.
• A torch (flashlight) and batteries.
• A first-aid kit that includes a pair of scissors, tweezers, a good supply of band-aids and disinfectant.
• Oral rehydration salts for diarrhoea or sunstroke.
• Antihistamine pills for insect bites and allergies.
• Antiseptic and antibacterial cream – cuts and abrasions may fester in the tropics.
• Any regular medication you are taking.
• Water purification tablets in case you need to drink from rivers in the wild (if so, drink from running water in streams and rivers).
• Cash, preferably US$ in lower denominations (maximum $50). In smaller cities, cash is king.

Part One: Planning your trip

Within Brazil, local operators can be cheaper as many international operators subcontract with them. Check that an English-speaking guide will be available before you start.

Cia Nacional de Ecoturismo (www.ciaecoturismo.com.br) offers customized packages for almost any of the national parks of Brazil, but the English version of the website is shaky.

Banani (www.banani.com.br) is based in Rio, offers a range of products and welcomes families with kids.

Natureco (www.natureco.com.br) operates out of the Mato Grosso and has an excellent package offering three biomes in one: the Pantanal, the Amazon and the Cerrado.

Terra Nativa Ecoturismo (www.terranativa.com.br) has a more scientific approach to its tours with tour guides who are biology, history and botany specialists. They have special programmes for international and gap-year students.

Adventure Club (www.adventureclub.com.br) (in Portuguese) has excursions in almost all the national parks described here. Email: karina@adventureclub.com.br for English bookings.

Freeway Brasil (www.freeway.tur.br) should be commended for having several packages for people with disabilities and special needs.

Biosfera Brasil (www.biosferabrasil.com) offers tours in many national parks, with some options designed specifically for women, the elderly or gay men.

Activities
Bird-watching
The extensive wetlands of the Pantanal are heaven for birdwatchers who have been singing the area's praises for decades. It is well nigh impossible to miss the most obvious species, from the jabiru stork to the wattled jacanã, even during a casual jungle walk. The Atlantic forest and Iguaçu national parks are also areas with easily observable avifauna. The Amazon, due to the density of its

Brazilian Wildlife

This wildlife is impressive: out of approximately 250,000 plant species that exist worldwide, 55,000 can be found in Brazil, including the largest collection of palm trees (359 species) and orchids (2300 species at the last count). Brazil's forests provide shelter for 15% of the world's birds and for 10% of all existing amphibians. Brazil contains 394 mammal species of which 96 are endemic (occurring naturally only in the country) including the greatest assortment of primates on Earth, with 55 distinct species.

vegetation, is less so, but its sheer size ensures that there are also many good observation spots.

Birding.com (www.birding.com.br) is a Brazilian company based in Manaus offering birding expeditions in the Amazon and the Pantanal.

Pantanal Bird Club (www.geocities.com/thetropics/cabana/6292) organizes bird-finding tours in Brazil's most productive areas.

Field Guides (www.fieldguides.com) specializes in bird tours worldwide and can handle arrangements for private trips.

Finally, there are several Cerrado private reserves specializing in bird-watching:
www.reservabacupari.com.br
www.valedasararas.com.br
www.chapadaveadeiros.com.br

Right: The Wattled Jacana looks clumsy but it can balance very well on the broad-leafed aquatic plants of the Brazilian lakes and rivers.

Part One: Planning your trip

Fishing

The varied species of the Amazon and its tributaries present the discriminating angler with numerous challenges, but the Pantanal and Bonito can also satisfy the most ardent enthusiast.

High Hook Fishing Tours (www.fishinginamazon.com) offers experienced sport fishing in the Amazon and the Xingu.

Amazon Tours (www.amazontours.com) specializes in fishing the popular *tucunaré* (peacock bass) on the Rio Negro.

Every private *fazenda* in the Pantanal offers fishing options.

Caving

Caves in Brazil tend to be mostly horizontal and thus easy to explore and visit with basic equipment, if any. The best places for caving are in the Cerrado, and the Chapadas of Diamantina and Guimarães. There are also many easily accessible caves in São Paulo state and in the region of Bonito (Pantanal).

Eco-Brazil (www.ecobrazil.com) has adventure and trekking tours rated from easy to difficult that include some excellent caving activities.

Diving

Brazil's extensive coast offers many opportunities for diving and snorkelling, with the best options in the northeast, especially in the archipelagoes of Fernando de Noronha and Abrolhos. There are three main dive operators on the island:

Águas Claras: www.aguasclaras-fn.com.br/novo
Atlantis Divers: www.atlantisdivers.com.br
Noronha Divers: www.noronhadivers.com.br

Some excellent diving opportunities exist not far from Rio de Janeiro in Ilha Grande and Angra dos Reis with a dozen shipwrecks and underwater caves. The website www.ilhagrande.com.br contains a list of scuba operators on the island.

Bahia Scuba (www.bahiascuba.com.br) is a site in Portuguese offering scuba diving in the state of Bahia.

Photography

Trilhas & Trilhas in São Paulo offers adventures specializing in photography.
Website: www.trilhasetrilhas.tur.br (in Portuguese),
Email: contato@trilhasetrilhas.tur.br
Tel: (11) 6231-2933 or
(11) 6231-0840.
Edson Endrigo is a professional bird photographer and English-speaking guide who specializes in the Mata Atlântica.
Website: www.avesfoto.com.br

Introduction

Jungle Survival

Alaya Viagens E Turismo
(www.alaya.com.br) offers
survival training courses in the
Atlantic rainforest.
Jungletrekker
(www.dtvisions.com/jungle
trekker/english/index.html) is unique
with its 'Jungle Survival Academies' in
the Amazon rainforest (including in
the difficult-to-reach Jaú
National Park) and home-stay
programmes with local families.

Golfing

There are many golf courses and clubs in Brazil. Here are the ones you are most likely to combine with a visit to a national park:

Amazon

Manaus Country Club
Address: Estrada Belém, 3000 – Colônia Cachoeira Grande
Tel: (55 92) 644-2995
Email: mcountryclub@uol.com.br

Mata Atlântica

Near Tijuca
Gávea Golf and Country Club
Address: Estrada da Gávea 800, São Conrado
Rio de Janeiro
Tel: (021) 3323-6050
Email: gaveagolf@gaveagolf.com.br

Near Serra dos Orgãos
Teresópolis Golf Club
Address: Avenida Franklin Roosevelt, 2222 – Teresópolis
Tel: (55 21) 2742-1691
Email: teregolf@terenet.com.br

Iguaçu

Iguaçu Golf Club and Resort
Address: Av. das Cataratas, 6845 Foz de Iguaçu
Email: iguassugolf@iguassugolf.com.br

Cerrado

Clube de Golfe de Brasília
Address: Setor de Clubes Esportivos Sul – Trecho 2 – Lote 2, Brasília
Tel: (55 61) 224-2718 / (55 61) 223-7194
Website: www.golfebrasilia.com.br

Pinheráis

Clube Curitibano
Address: Av. 25 de Janeiro, 2461 Curitiba
Tel: (55 41) 672-1474 / (55 41) 672-3355

Part One: Planning your trip

Trekking

Trekking in Brazil ensures that you see the country off the beaten path with none of the tail-to-tail trailing behind a fellow walker which often happens in more developed regions. However, tracks are not always discernible and mobile phones do not work in remote areas, so do not travel alone and always hire a local guide. You may not have a choice: IBAMA insists that for certain parks you are only allowed in with local, certified guides, who can be hired for about R$50–60 per day (the price is for a group).

Brazil Adventure International (www.brazadv.com) offers some inspiring and varied hiking tours in the southeastern Atlantic rainforest in Itatiaia and Serra da Bocaína national parks.

Amazon Adventures (www.amazonadventures.com/brazil.htm) has excellent walking tours in some out-of-the-way national parks, including Chapada Diamantina, Serra da Capivara and Lençóis Maranhenses.

Venturas & Aventuras (www.venturas.com.br) offers many interesting walking expeditions in about 10 different national parks.

Extreme sports

If you are an adrenaline junkie, it is possible to go mountain biking, surfing, kayaking, canyoning or rafting in parks where infrastructure is more developed.

Make sure your travel insurance explicitly covers any activity you sign for.

There are extreme sports in several of Brazil's national parks, including Iguaçu, Tijuca and Cipó. Visit www.bikehike.com/brazil/brazil.html for more information.

Aurora Eco (www.auroraeco.com.br) based in São Paulo has personalized activities ranging from mountain biking in the Southern Grasslands to kayaking in the Amazon.

City Dangers

It is worth remembering that the overwhelming majority of visitors to Brazil have a trouble-free, enjoyable holiday. However, levels of violence are high in the big cities, especially in São Paulo and Rio de Janeiro, so be streetwise and extra vigilant after dark. Carry identification on yourself all the time; a photocopy of the passport page with your picture on will suffice, sometimes even for changing money or for checking into a hotel. If there is a hotel safe (*cofre*) available in your room, use it to store any valuables. Do not take much cash or any jewellery at all to the beach. It is advisable to sit at a chair provided by a *barraca* (a beach hut) and ask the attendant to look after your towel and clothes.

Introduction

Giants of the Amazon Rainforest

The Amazon is home to:
The green anaconda – the most massive snake in the world, up to 8–9m (26–29ft) long with a girth like that of a man.
The victoria regia – the biggest water lily in the world with a leaf up to 3m (10ft) in diameter.
The capybara – the biggest rodent in the world, up to 1.3m (4ft) in length.
The arran turtle – the biggest river turtle in the world, 90cm (35 in) in length and weighing 45kg (99 lb).
The giant otter – the biggest otter in the world, up to 1.4m (4.5ft) in length.

Some would also add the pirarucu, which is one of the largest freshwater fish in the world, with a body nearing 3m (10ft) and weighing 200kg (441 lb). However, the largest river fish ever caught was a Mekong giant catfish back in 2005 in Thai waters.

PART TWO: ECO ISSUES AND CLIMATE
Brazilian biomes
Amazon rainforest (Amazônia)

The Amazon rainforest biome covers 4,000,000km^2 (1,544,000 sq miles) – around 47% of Brazil – in the states of Acre, Amazonas, Roraima, Amapá, Rondônia, Pará, Maranhão, Piauí and Upper Mato Grosso do Norte. The climate is hot equatorial and extremely humid. Rainfall decreases progressively from around 3500mm (138 in) at the bottom of the Andes to 1500mm (59 in) at the mouth of the Amazon River. On the plus side, although spanning the Equator, evaporation from the rainforest keeps the temperatures milder than expected, ranging from 25–32°C (77–89°F).

An ancient lake called Belterra covered the area between two and 25 million years ago and its sediments were deposited in today's basin. As the earth's tectonic plates moved and the Andes rose, the lake disappeared and modern rivers began to excavate its bed dividing it into highlands, plains and depressions. These in turn determine whether an area becomes flooded or not and form the principal ecosystems of the biome.

Dry land (*terra firme*) constitutes the majority of the Amazon rainforest. This is forest that is never flooded, spread across a plain of up to 100–200m (328–656ft) in altitude and reaching to the bottom of the Andes. The soil is poor in nutrients and can not be cultivated easily. The trees here stock up with natural fertilizers through nitrogen-fixing bacteria in their roots; it is because the trees carry the nutrients with them, so to speak, that regeneration of a disappearing rainforest is well nigh impossible.

Várzea is land periodically flooded by the muddy waters of the Amazon itself and its large tributaries, the so-called 'white rivers' that flow from the Andes, deposit minerals and turn the area highly fertile. It is this ecosystem that allowed the existence of an indigenous human population in the pre-colonial era. The rivers are rich in fish (there are 2400 species in the Amazon River system), with aquatic mammals such as pink river dolphins, manatees and giant otters. Aquatic birds like herons, ducks and jacanas predominate.

The *Igapó* ecosystem is periodically flooded by either the

Part Two: Eco issues and climate

'clear-water' rivers that descend from the acidic soils of the central highlands (*planalto central*) towards the north, such as the Rio Tapajós and the Xingu, or by 'black' rivers that descend from the swamps of the Guianas south, like the Rio Negro, whose waters are dark from the decomposing vegetation and are as low in minerals as rainwater. Both types are low in nutrients so, unlike the *várzea*, the flora and fauna of this ecosystem are poorer.

Above: *The Amazon River snakes through the rainforest in an ever-changing course that depends on periodic flooding.*

There are several national parks in the Amazônia biome, but many are inaccessible by road or require a permit. The main exception is Jaú, which can be reached by boat from Manaus, the capital of the state of Amazonas. It was inscribed as a UNESCO Natural Heritage Site in 2000 and expanded in 2003 to its current area, plus a surrounding Central Amazon Conservation Complex to a total of 60,000km^2 (23,160 sq miles). However, the undeveloped nature of Amazônia ensures that even day-trippers who venture outside the main cities can be assured of a rewarding rainforest experience.

Cerrado

As the Amazon basin turns to the *planalto central* (200–1700m/ 656–5578ft) that occupies the states of Tocantins, Middle Mato Grosso do Norte, Goiás, Eastern Mato Grosso do Sul and Western Minas Gerais, the Amazon rainforest gives way to the Cerrado, which is highly reminiscent of the large African savannas. This is the second largest biome, comprising 20% of the Brazilian territory.

Introduction

Since trees are widely spaced and stunted, an observer might be led to think that lack of water is the reason, but this is not the case: the soil contains sufficient humidity. The odd appearance of the Cerrado trees and bushes, with twisted, rickety trunks and bulky, firm leaves, reveals the excessive acidity and occasional toxicity of the soil that contains large amounts of aluminium. The dry season – a relative concept in the rainforest – is quite pronounced here and runs from May to September. This is when periodic forest fires occur that clear large areas but allow the resprouting and regeneration of the vegetation. This ranges from

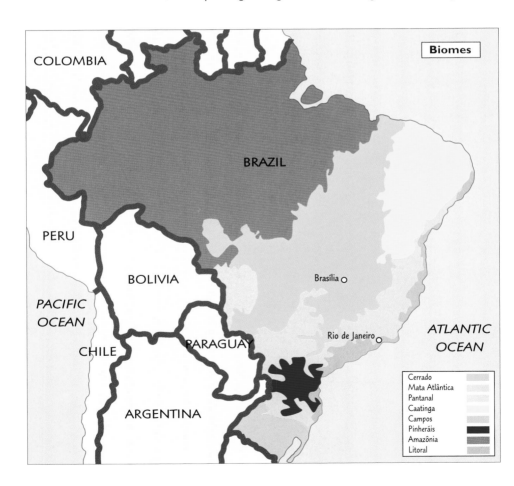

Biomes

COLOMBIA

BRAZIL

PERU

BOLIVIA

Brasília ○

PACIFIC OCEAN

PARAGUAY

Rio de Janeiro ○

CHILE

ATLANTIC OCEAN

ARGENTINA

Cerrado
Mata Atlântica
Pantanal
Caatinga
Campos
Pinheráis
Amazônia
Litoral

Part Two: Eco issues and climate

transitional lowland rainforest vegetation (*cerradão*), open grassland (*campo limpo*), fields covered with sparse shrubs and small trees (*campo sujo*), plants growing on rocky outcrops (*campo rupestre*), open (*vereda*) and closed gallery forest (*mata da galeria*) plus copses of palm trees on river embankments (*mata ciliar*).

Because of such variety, the Cerrado is one of the two major Brazilian biodiversity hotspots with a rich and easily observable wildlife. This is where you will find anteaters, maned wolves, big cats, deer and giant armadillos. Deep canyons, waterfalls and amazing rock formations make the national parks of this biome some of the most pleasant and worthwhile in Brazil. In 2001, the Emas and Chapada dos Veadeiros national parks were inscribed on the UNESCO World Heritage List.

Caatinga

Further towards the northeastern states of Ceará, Piauí, Rio Grande do Norte, Pernambuco, Alagoas, Paraíba and Bahia, the absence of rivers and rain turns the landscape into dry, thorny scrubland where water is scarce. This is the Caatinga biome, comprising about 11% of the Brazilian territory, and characterized by a desert climate, very high temperatures, low humidity, irregular rainfall and dry vegetation. Unlike the Cerrado, the soil here is fertile and it is the absence of water that has turned the area into a semi-arid desert. Wherever it has been possible to irrigate it – damming the Rio São Francisco, for instance – garden vegetables and fruit such as grapes and melons have been grown in abundance.

The national and state parks in the Caatinga are Brazil's most enigmatic, with rock carvings that have not been adequately explained or researched. Notably, the most representative park of the Caatinga, the Serra da Capivara, was inscribed on the UNESCO World Heritage List in 1991 for its cultural significance rather than its natural beauty.

Life is hard in the Caatinga but the flora and fauna have adapted well to the heat and aridity of the region. Cactuses abound; plants are mostly spiny and vascular; and animals tend to be nocturnal, with a high proportion of lizards, snakes and small mammals.

Plants of Special Interest

Rosewood
Brazilwood
Curare
Brazil nut
Quinine
Rubber tree
Guaraná
Urucum
Monkey puzzle tree
Açaí palm
Giant waterlily

Introduction

Pantanal

The Pantanal biome is located in the basin of the Upper Paraguay River. This is the largest area of freshwater marshes in the world, shared among Brazil, Bolivia and Paraguay. Although it comprises only about 2% of the Brazilian territory, native vegetation still covers 97% of its area and, as a result, the abundance of its animal life and diversity of its vegetation are spectacular.

Unlike the Amazon where the rainforest hides the wildlife very expertly, the flat landscape with low-lying bush, streams and ponds renders this by far the best region to see animals in Brazil. In particular, as with all wetlands, the bird life is just stunning. Over 650 species of birds alone have been identified, as well as over 110 species of mammals, 50 of reptiles, and 242 of fish. One can hardly fail to spot caimans, macaws, howler monkeys, peccaries, armadillos, anacondas and, if lucky, nocturnal predators such as the jaguar. A biosphere reserve that includes the Pantanal Matogrossense National Park was inscribed on the UNESCO World Heritage List in 1981, but private reserves in the region provide easier and better animal viewing opportunities.

Below: Bromeliad epiphytes in the forest canopy hold rainwater in their stems and serve as pools of water to birds and primates alike.

Atlantic rainforest (Mata Atlântica)

Brazil's other, relatively unknown, rainforest (Mata Atlântica) stretches for about 4000km (2486 miles) along the Atlantic coast of Brazil from the state of Rio Grande do Norte to Rio Grande do Sul, comprising coastal Bahia, Espirito Santo, Eastern Minas Geráis, São Paulo and the whole of the state of Rio de Janeiro – all in all about 15% of the country's area. Five centuries of colonization, agriculture and urbanization have resulted in the Mata Atlântica becoming Brazil's most devastated biome; only 8% of the original rainforest remains. More so than the Amazon or the Cerrado, the Atlantic rainforest is among the top five biodiversity hotspots on earth. This exceptional biodiversity is due to its

Part Two: Eco issues and climate

tropical and subtropical position, proximity to the sea and substantial differences in altitude. It is here, in the Serra do Mar and the Serra da Mantiqueira, that the highest peaks on the Atlantic side of the whole American continent can be found. Because of this, its ecosystems, species composition and structure change with altitude. At sea level there is lowland rainforest mixed with marine ecosystems such as mangrove swamps and *restingas* (sandbanks); giant trees and palms colonized by epiphytes such as orchids and bromeliads occupy the submontane and montane sections up to 1000m (3281ft); a permanently misty cloud forest characterizes the range between 1000m (3281ft) and 1800m (5906ft); and finally the altitude fields above 1800m (5906ft) are dominated by grasslands.

With its proximity to the big urban centres of the southeast and its cooler temperatures (18–24°C/64–75°F), the Mata Atlântica is the most visited nature area of Brazil. Apart from the richness of wildlife, the sudden rise of the mountains from the coast has exceptional scenic value, as anyone who has visited the city of Rio de Janeiro can attest. Deeper inland, the edge of the rainforest by the Rio Paraná forms the best-known park of South America: the famous Iguaçu Falls.

In 1999 all Mata Atlântica reserves in the southeast and in the Discovery Coast of Brazil were declared World Heritage Sites by UNESCO.

Pine forests (Pinheráis) and Southern grasslands (Campos)

The Mata Atlântica comes to an end in the southern states of Paraná and Santa Catarina with the subtropical Pinheráis ecosystem, sometimes promoted to a fully fledged biome, where tropical and temperate flora coexist. Araucaria pine forests were once predominant but today they cover less than 10% of their original area.

Campos continues on all the way into Uruguay, encompassing most of the state of Rio Grande do Sul and, along with Pinheráis, accounts for about 2.5% of Brazil's area. The climate is mild to temperate, very humid, with no dry season and the region consists of gently rolling hills covered with subtropical grasslands

Brazil

Brazil's landmass – the fifth largest of any country – stands at 8,511,965km² (3,285,619 sq miles) dominating the South American continent. The best-known of its geological features is the famed Amazon Basin, with its thick and still unexplored rainforest, where anthropologists estimate that 10–20 tribes live untouched by the 21st century. The remote Amazon is not, however, the be-all and end-all of what Brazil has to offer, and visitors will be pleased to learn that all of its ecosystems have representative parks that are both accessible and manageable: for instance, there are three major ones within an hour or two's drive out of Rio de Janeiro. Furthermore, because of the unspoiled, unpopulated and undeveloped expanses of biomes such as the Amazon, the Pantanal or the Cerrado, it is still possible to appreciate the wildlife or scenery simply by travelling in the region.

Introduction

(as opposed to their continuation in Argentina, the temperate grasslands known as *pampas*, which are cooler and drier). Like the Mata Atlântica, this biome is disappearing rapidly because of the intensification of agriculture, drainage of wetlands and conversion of empty land into grazing pastures. Visitors are compensated with one of the best of Brazil's national parks, the Aparados da Serra, in the northern borders of the southern grasslands mixed with the southern pine forests of the Mata Atlântica.

Coastal regions and islands (Litoral)

The long, thin coastal biome (about 0.5% of Brazil's area) is composed of many ecosystems: estuaries, mangroves, lagoons, sand dunes, beaches, rocky outcrops, and islands from the Amazon to Uruguay. This is where 50% of the population live with a density (87 per km^2) six times higher than the country's average (17 per km^2). As one might expect, pollution and industrialization have made a major, negative impact and fragmented the coastal ecology. The largest contiguous part of this biome is found on the northeastern coast from below the Amazon to northern Bahia. It is also the most spectacular, with reefs, variegated sand dunes, remote beaches like the famous Jericoacoara and the archipelago of Fernando de Noronha.

Environmental problems

Brazil's size has magnified its environmental issues which have become global and affect us all. The biggest and most discussed is deforestation. After Russia and Canada, Brazil is the most forested country in the world, but only around 3,000,000km^2 (1,158,000 sq miles) of the estimated original 5,000,000km^2 (1,930,000 sq miles) of cover remain. Most of the depletion has been in the Mata Atlântica out of which only 80,000km^2 (30,880 sq miles) are still standing. Only 20% of the original Cerrado cover remains, the rest of the land having been turned into cotton, sugar cane or soya plantations. The fight is on to ensure the Amazon rainforest does not suffer the same fate. An area the size of France has already been lost there, most of it in the last 25 years, as deforestation has accelerated. In 1988–89 alone 17,860km^2 (6894 sq miles) were cleared compared with the previous decade's total of 21,000km^2 (8106 sq miles). This trend has unfortunately continued at an average of 15,000km^2 (5790 sq miles) per year – about half the size of Belgium.

Part Two: Eco issues and climate

Gold prospectors (*garimpeiros*) are to blame for some of the environmental destruction that includes pollution of rivers with heavy metals, but there are also 2000 timber extraction companies – including two dozen multinationals, mostly from Asia – that operate in the Amazon legally and illegally. More significantly, the government of Brazil itself, with its agrarian reform policy has been encouraging the 'liberation' of Amazônia and the migration of the city poor to individual farms in the interior. There they are offered incentives to cultivate soya, a crop the state governments believe can kick-start another economic boom.

0061530 3
Limerick
County Library

The other major eco-problem is the desertification of the northeast. An area larger than Scotland is rapidly drying out, as the Caatinga slowly progresses. The complex reasons for this have to do with human activity, global warming and gradual loss of soil fertility. The situation is so grave that the government has earmarked US$2 billion to try and reverse the trend with the reintroduction of native plants that can help fight erosion and by irrigation. The huge Rio São Francisco dam project in the borders of Bahia and Pernambuco is part of this plan.

Below: *Rainforest devastation caused by slash-and-burn techniques.*

THE AMAZON RAINFOREST

Although vast, the Amazon is the most inaccessible area of Brazil. It is reached normally via a flight to Manaus, the 'gateway to the rainforest', that stands on the confluence with the Rio Negro. Other urban centres are Santarém and Belém in the mouth of the Amazon. One can travel between them (and beyond, all the way to Iquitos, Peru) by boat, but they are all very hard to reach by road.

There are many jungle lodges in the vicinity of Manaus that offer jungle trips for all budgets. However, as it has now become increasingly more feasible to travel to Jaú National Park, it is worth making the trip. This is the largest national park in Brazil and the one with the largest primary tropical rainforest in the world. It is a low-lying tableland (0–200m/0–656ft) separated by periodically flooded valleys, delineated by 'white' rivers of silt and arenite, such as the Rio Carabinani in the south and the Rio Paunini flowing into the Rio Unini in the north, and the 'black' Rio Negro in the east. The interior of the park is criss-crossed by the Rio Papagaio, the Rio Guariba and the Rio Jaú that lie wholly within the park.

Amazon Ecosystems

Terra firme dense forest represents about 70% of Jaú National Park, with Brazil nut trees (*Bertholletia excelsa*), Angelins (*Pithecellobium racemosum*), Quarubas (*Vochysia maxima*) and Sucupiras (*Diplotropis purpurea*). In the northeast of the park where there are higher altitudes, the more common trees are the Mangarana (*Microphalis guianensis*), the Sorva (*Couma guianensis*) and the Amapá (*Parahancornia amapa*). *Varzea* and riverine open forest represent around 12% where groves of Paxiúba (*Iriartea sp.*), Açaí (*Euterpe oleracea*) and Jauari palms (*Astrocaryum jauari*) predominate. Finally, *igapó* streams and rivers, where many species of orchid thrive, make up the rest.

Opposite, top to bottom:
Piranhas only attack the weak or bleeding; the Amazon jungle; a boto, or pink river dolphin, leaps out of the water.

The Amazon Rainforest

Park Statistics

Area: 22,720km² (8770 sq miles).
Rainfall: 2000–2250mm
(79–89 in) per year. The climate is
equatorial hot and humid.
Temperature: Throughout the year
the average is 25–27°C (77–81°F),
with a maximum of 38°C (100°F)
and a minimum of 12–14°C
(54–57°F).
Opening Times: There is an
IBAMA boat-office that doubles as a
visitor centre at the entrance to the
park on the confluence of the River
Jaú and the Rio Negro. Entry costs
R$3, and the park is open from
07:00–18:00.
Note: Manaus and the state of
Amazonas are one hour behind
Rio/São Paulo.

Parque Nacional do Jaú
Best time to go

It may sound strange, but the park closes occasionally during the dry season which runs from November to March. This is because river levels can become too low for navigation by speedboat (*voadeira*). The best time to visit is just before the onset of the dry season, September to November, and in June/July, just after the onset of the rainy season. If the park is open, you should expect some rain, so wrap your cameras and any electrical equipment in plastic with water-absorbing desiccants such as silica gel.

How to get there

The easiest way of reaching Jaú is by boat. There are express speedboats to Novo Airão that depart daily from the port of Manaus at 15:00 (about four hours). There are also cheaper but slower boats that leave towards Barcelos throughout the day and take 18 hours. If driving a car, take the state highway AM-070 (from the opposite side of Manaus) to Manacapuru and then the AM-352 at Km 80. After Manacapuru, the road is not paved. There is also a bus that runs from Manaus twice a day, leaving from the opposite bank to the port.

You need a permit from IBAMA, whose address in Manaus is Rua Ministro João Gonçalves de Sousa 1km (0.4 miles) outside Manaus on the BR-319 highway. Tel: (92) 3613-3277, fax: (92) 3613-3095.

Your best bet is to go to the state tourism kiosk at Manaus airport, where they can advise you on whether the park is open and give you addresses of operators or guides who offer trips. If you arrive in the middle of the night (all too common) and the counter is closed, the main information centre is at Rua Saldanha Marinho 321. Tel: (92) 3233-1928/1095.

What to see
Inside the park

The park is best explored by *voadeira*, which relies on water levels being high, but on a few walks it is possible to see three impressive waterfalls. Just by the entrance, you can see the waterfall of the Igarapé Preto (best between the months of October and January).

Parque Nacional do Jaú

Further beyond there is a short trail by the Rio Carabinari that leads to another waterfall, the Cachoeira Guariba. The Jaú waterfall, about 90 minutes away from the entrance, is really a set of rapids that is negotiated only by speedboat when levels are high.

You will very likely fish for food, especially if you are camping over a period of a few days. Many of the species found in the Amazon are here, such as the jaú (*Paulicea lutkeni*) which has given its name to the park; the peacock bass or tucunaré (*Cichla ocellaris*), much prized by anglers; the infamous piranha; and the giant pirarucu (*Arapaima gigas*), one the largest river fish in the world. Up to 3m (10ft) in length and two tons in weight, it is so large that it could not be caught by the pre-discovery Indians until metal hooks were introduced by the Europeans.

The less accessible Paunini and Unini rivers that form the north boundary of the park are loosely populated. Much closer to the park entrance, a trail leads to the small community of Seringalzinho on the Rio Jaú. These are caboclos, namely Portuguese-speaking descendants of Europeans and Indians who now form the majority of people who live in the rainforest, there being very few pure-bred Indians left. Families sometimes agree to accommodate visitors who wish to experience the local subsistence way of life that consists of hunting, fishing and the cultivation of manioc flour.

Anavilhanas

Just before you reach the park coming from Manaus, you will find the Anavilhanas Ecological Station, in one of the many archipelagos in the Amazon. It runs over 100km (62 miles) along the Rio Negro and comprises 400 islands with an area of 3500km² (1351 sq miles) populated by spider and howler monkeys, giant otters, pumas, jaguars, black caimans, both kinds of river dolphins and 350 fish species. There are riverboat excursions from Manaus that can combine with Jaú National Park.

Mariuá Archipelago

A good day trip from Jaú is to the Mariuá Archipelago, on the Rio Negro, 170km (106 miles) north of the park. This is the largest fluvial archipelago in the world with over 1200 islands. Almost 200

Tour Operators

There are operators in Manaus who offer a trip to Jaú (prices depend on the number of people taking part).
Fontur operates from within Hotel Tropical, tel: (92) 3658-3052/3438, website: www.fontur.com.br
Eco Discovery Tours, Rua dos Andradas 464, first floor, Manaus-Center, tel: (92) 3082-4732 / (92) 3234-4737, website: www.eco-discovery-tours.com
Nature Safaris, Rua Flávio Espírito Santo 1 Kyssia, 2, Planalto, tel: (92) 3622-2577, website: www.selvatur.com.br

One advantage of using these operators is that they will normally obtain your permit for you.

Accommodation

There is no infrastructure in the park and you will need to lodge at **Novo Airão**, unless you are camping inside the park.
Josely, João Paulo II 1027, tel: (92) 365-1157 – 12 rooms with aircon, TV and mini bar.
Rio Negro, Av. Castelo Branco (no number), tel: (92) 365-1102 – 14 rooms, more basic.

The Amazon Rainforest

Accommodation Inside Manaus

Tropical Manaus: Built in 1976, this is the luxury option 16km (10 miles) outside Manaus in the river beach of Ponta Negra. There is a 'resort' part and a 'hotel' part. Av. Coronel Teixeira 1320, tel: (92) 3659-5000, www.tropicalhotel.com.br

Taj Mahal: In the centre of town, with a revolving restaurant, sauna, tennis court and pool. Av. Getúlio Vargas, 741, tel: (92) 3627-3737, www.grupotajmahal.com.br

Slaass: Offers apartments with cooking facilities at the price of a hotel room. Av. Senador Álvaro Maia 1442, tel: (92) 3633-3520, www.slaashotel.com.br

Brasil: Cheaper, comfortable. Av. Getúlio Vargas, 657, tel: (92) 233-6575.

Iberostar Grand Amazon: You may wish to sleep on a boat that undertakes cruises on the Amazon and the Rio Negro. The boat leaves Manaus on Thursdays and Sundays. Phone reservations are made centrally through Spain (+34) 922 070300, www.iberostar.com.br

species of fish live there, including many ornamental fish exported around the world. It is a tropical paradise of walks on fine sandy beaches, and refreshing swimming in the dark waters of the Rio Negro.

Novo and Velho Airão

Surprisingly, the city of Novo Airão has itself an attraction to offer: its people are still involved in shipbuilding the old-fashioned way. There are two factories in the area which you can visit and be transported centuries back to the old Portuguese methods of constructing Amazonian boats.

Finally, there is also Velho Airão. During the rubber boom between 1880 and 1910 this city was awash with immigrant labour but the decline of the rubber trade caused the place to be abandoned (its people moving to Novo Airão). The jungle has now reclaimed it, and it has become an attraction in itself, an atmospheric ghost town only a slight detour from the park entrance.

Manaus and vicinity

Every visitor to the Amazon should allow at least two to three days to see the city of Manaus which offers some of the few cultural and architectural points of interest in the area.

At the top of any itinerary should be the neoclassical **Teatro Amazonas** in Praça São Sebastião, a symbol of the rubber boom, built in 1896 at the height of the Amazonian *belle époque*. Guided visits Monday–Saturday 09:00–16:00, R$10.

The **Mercado Municipal** (Town Market) building, dating from an even earlier era (1883), with its hustle and bustle, is another unmissable treat and was reopened in 2007 after a long renovation (Rua dos Bares 46, free, 08:00–18:00).

The **Seringal Vila Paraíso Museum**, 40m (44 yards) by boat across the Rio Negro, utilizes an old film set that illustrates in great detail the life of the rubber barons and tappers of the late 19th century (Wednesday–Sunday, R$5 entry or R$12 including boat transfer).

Birds of the Amazon

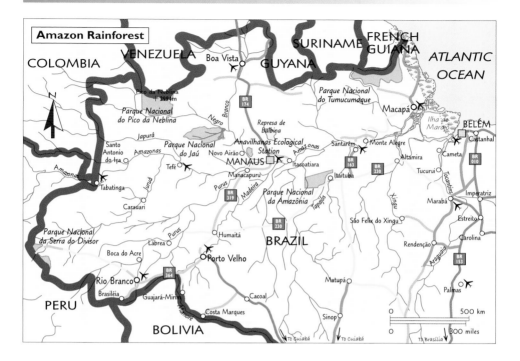

You can opt to stay inside the town, or in the jungle resorts that have sprung up around the city for a more comfortable, but always satisfactory, jungle experience.

Birds of the Amazon

About 700 bird species are found in the Amazon and you don't have to go too far from Manaus to observe them. Some of them – such as the Guianan Cock-of-the-Rock' (*Rupicola rupicola*) and the Screaming Piha (*Lipaugus vociferans*), the 'voice of Amazonia' – are iconic symbols of the region; some like the Musician Wren (*Cyphorhinus aradus*) are sought out for their melodious singing and some, like the Hoatzin (*Opisthocomus hoazin*), have evolved into myth.

The elusive cock-of-the-rock is a head-turner of a bird with a bright Day-Glo orange plumage and a fan-like crest. These birds are solitary and elusive but congregate together during the mating

The Amazon Rainforest

Bird Life

Close to the Anavilhanas is the Igarapé das Araras, ideal for observing bird life. Here you can spot **Red-billed Toucans**; **Black Skimmers**, tern-like birds with sharp, dagger-like beaks; **Turquoise Tanagers**; **Brazilian Cormorants**; **Large-billed Terns** and **Thrush-like Wrens** – both threatened species; **Red-and-green Macaws**; **Capped** and **Little Blue Herons**; the fly-catching **White-throated Kingbirds**; **Long-billed Woodcreepers**; the loud and raucous **Tui Parakeets**; and **Red-breasted Blackbirds** which, belying their names, are a type of meadowlark.

season in special open courtship arenas called *leks*. There, males proudly display their plumage during a communal mating ritual and the less ornate brownish females watch the spectacle and choose their mates accordingly. The females then build their nests together on steep rocks and cliffs – hence the name – where they raise their young without any help from the males.

This is a species that exhibits bisexual behaviour. Young undeveloped males, one to two years old, also appear in the *lek* but select males whom they mount; in fact, they have been observed chasing off females to couple with the males themselves. They then disappear for a year until they re-emerge with the bright adult plumage to present themselves at the *lek* to pair off with females and be mounted, in turn, by younger males.

Like the cock-of-the-rock, the screaming piha belongs to the cotinga family. It emits a unique, ear-piercing wolf-whistle which sounds like 'Fri-Frio', giving the bird its local, colloquial name. Any visitor who stays in the rainforest for more than a few hours can hardly miss its call, but spotting the well-camouflaged bird itself, dark grey with a mottled throat and breast, is a more difficult proposition.

No one can accuse the musician wren of screaming – it has a distinctive, complex, almost choirboy-sounding song line that is renowned in the Amazon and beyond. According to local lore, when it decides to sing, all other birds stop their twittering and listen reverentially. The composer Olivier Messiaen was so taken with this bird that he incorporated its melody as a leitmotif for woodwinds in his work *Et exspecto resurrectionem mortuorum* (In Expectation of a Resurrection After Death).

The bird, however, that everyone wants to spot is the hoatzin, a bird so unlike any other that it is claimed to be the missing link between dinosaurs and birds: a new taxonomic order had to be established to accommodate it in biology. It looks like a red-brown perching pheasant with a long neck, small blue face and a spiky crest. What distinguishes it from other birds is the way it digests its food. Like a cow or a sheep it uses bacteria to break down vegetable matter such as leaves; this, however,

Amazon versus Nile

happens not in the gut, as in ruminants, but in a special enlarged compartment of its oesophagus. As a result of this fermentation, the birds stink of decomposition and are not hunted for food. The sounds they emit are also unbirdlike, resembling more the grunts and growls of mammals. But despite all this quirkiness, the scientific excitement emanated from the fact that the chicks are born with two claws at the tip of each wing. As the hoatzin nest is built on a branch overhanging standing water, the chicks dive in when threatened and use these claws to climb up to the safety of their nest once the danger has disappeared. It is those claws, which remind ornithologists of the *Archaeopteryx* fossils, that have precipitated a still unresolved debate about a 'living dinosaur relic'.

Amazon versus Nile

Which is the world's longest river? Surprisingly, the debate is still going on. And the first question is: where does it start? The source of the Nile was originally considered to be in Lake Victoria, but the Kargera feeder river starting in Rwanda's Nyungwe Forest (the 'true' source of the Nile) added another 480km (298 miles) to its length, making it a total of 6695km (4160 miles). This search for the source of the Nile was the Victorian explorers' Holy Grail, yet the search for the source of the Amazon has been much more complex and heated. The Rio Marañon, a tributary that joins the

Left: A male Guianan Cock-of-the-rock's mating rituals are some of the most complex in the animal kingdom.

The Amazon Rainforest

Amazon at Iquitos, Peru, starts at Lake Lauricocha and it was this that was considered the Amazon's source. However, detailed aerial photography led to a 1971 National Geographic expedition to the Andean glaciers of the Nevado Mismi massif. There, at an altitude of 5249m (17,223ft), following a series of small creeks, they arrived at the small Laguna McIntyre – named after the American Captain Loren McIntyre, the expedition's photographer – which is now accepted as the source of the Amazon.

Still, having established the source of the Amazon, the arguments continued. Which course do you take downstream? Unlike the Nile, flooding reshapes the Amazon from year to year. Even if this question is solved, up pops another. How do you arrive at its end, since there is a delta 275km (171 miles) wide at its mouth, forming an island, Marajó, the size of Switzerland? There is one school of geographers who measure the Amazon via the Breves channel to Cape Maguarinho on Marajó Island. This route is 6790km (4219 miles) and longer than the Nile, but the majority now agree to measure it further north to Ilha Bailique via the Canal do Norte which makes it 6490km (4033 miles). What is not in dispute though, is the immensity of the Amazon hydrographical system. Some of its tributaries – Rio Madeira, Rio Negro, Tocantins, Juruá, Araguaia – are huge rivers over 2000km (1243 miles) themselves. They collectively drain an area of 7,045,000km^2 (2,719,370 sq miles) – almost the size of Australia – compared to the Nile's 2,870,000km^2 (1,107,820 sq miles). The average discharge to the sea is 220,000 cubic metres per second, compared to the Nile's 5100. No other river comes close – the Congo is a poor second with just one sixth of the Amazon's outflow. The surge is so powerful that the river's non-saline water can be winched up with a bucket up to 180km (112 miles) into the Atlantic and is so wide that, when the conditions are right, surfers can ride its waves at high tide in a phenomenon called *pororoca*.

Brazil's highest mountain

For more than 400 years, Brazil's highest mountain was assumed to be the Pico da Bandeira in the southeastern state of Espiritu Santo, standing at an altitude of 2889m (9479ft). In 1946, an American pilot flying low over some unexplored, inaccessible regions of the Amazon changed all that when he noticed an

Brazil's highest mountain

uncharted peak peeking out of the clouds. He had discovered the Pico da Neblina (Misty Peak) which, as its name suggests, had always been covered in fog. It wasn't long before the Pico da Bandeira was demoted to third place, when the country's second highest peak, the 31 de Março, was spotted nearby.

It is characteristic of the remoteness of the region that even their altitudes were not known exactly until the 1960s, when they were measured barometrically by the Brazilian Ministry of Foreign Affairs. These heights stood as such for 40 years – and were quoted in all books and guides – until, that is, the advent of a joint military/scientific expedition in 2004 that checked those measurements using satellite navigation and positioning technology and adjusted them downwards:

	Old height	Adjusted height
Pico da Neblina	3014.1m (9889ft)	2993.78m (9822.5ft)
31 de Março	2992.4m (9814.7ft)	2972.66m (9753.2ft)

Both peaks now lie within the confines of the Pico da Neblina National Park, which is closed to the general public. A special IBAMA permit (and a good reason) are required for entry.

Amazon plants

Launched on 5 May 1921, Chanel No. 5 was created by Ernest Beaux at the request of Coco Chanel and has since been one of the most successful aromas of all time. It is based on jasmine grown in Provence and on the essential oil of the Rosewood tree (*Aniba rosaeodora*) that is native to the Amazon. This oil that gives the perfume its odour is natural *linalo-ol* (also found in smaller quantities in basil), but it can only be extracted from the bark, which means the trees have to be chopped down. It is estimated that 500,000 such trees have been lost to the perfume industry and in April 1992 the rosewood was added to the endangered list by IBAMA. In 1997, French ecologists started a boycott campaign against Chanel products and as a result, a new, sustainable method of farming the trees is being overseen by the Brazilian government and a method of extracting the oil from the leaves has been developed.

Accommodation Around Manaus

Ariaú Jungle Tower: At the edge of Lake Ariaú in Iranduba, about 1hr 45min from Manaus. Minimum two nights, reservations only. Tel: (92) 2121-5000, www.ariau.com.br

Aldeia dos Lagos: On an island, 365km (227 miles) away from Manaus; 4–5hr away by car and by boat. Minimum four days. Tel: (92) 3248-9988, www.viverde.com.br/aldeia.html

Anavilhanas Lodge is the only option at the Anavilhanas archipelago, and a very good alternative to or in combination with Jaú National Park. Minimum four days. Reservations in the Manaus Shopping Centre, Av. Eduardo Ribeiro, 520, Sala 304, by phone (92) 3622-8996 or online at www.anavilhanaslodge.com

Flotel Piranha Rainforest Adventure Station: 1.5hrs away from Manaus by car plus 1hr by boat. It is set in a protected area. Minimum four days. Tel: (92) 3656-603, www.naturesafaris.com.br

Tiwa Amazonas Ecoresort: The closest hotel to Manaus, on the other bank of the Rio Negro. Tel: (92) 9995-7892, www.tiwa.com.br

Acajatuba Jungle Lodge: By the Rio Acajatuba, 3–4hr from Manaus by boat. Great value, minimum two days. Tel: (92) 3642-0358, www.acajatuba.com.br

The Amazon Rainforest

Amazon Species

Jaú National Park protects key threatened species, including the jaguar, the Amazonian manatee, the black caiman and two species of river dolphin. Other species found in the park are ocelots, giant otters, uacaris, capuchin and howler monkeys, tapirs, anacondas, deer, wild pigs, sloths, armadillos and agoutis, plus a large selection of birds including toucans, curassows, tinamous, macaws, harpy eagles and parrots. During the dry (or not-so-rainy) season the waters recede and sandy beaches start surfacing by the side of the rivers. Between November and January the 11 species of turtle such as the *jabuti* (Red-footed) Tortoise (*Geochelone carbonaria*) that live in the rivers come to these beaches to lay their eggs which are farmed by locals as they are considered a delicacy.

The rosewood is one of a number of trees native to the Amazon rainforest that has been commercially exploited, sometimes to near-extinction. The name of the country itself is a reference to the *pau-brasil* or Brazilwood tree (*Caesalpinia echinata*) that once thrived in the area; it was the first casualty of the Portuguese conquest, as it was traded for the highly valued red dye that could be extracted from its bark. Nowadays, it is endangered and you can see it in any quantity only in Bahia's Pau Brasil National Park that bears its name, or in the remote biospheres of the Amazon.

As local tribes passed on their knowledge to the Europeans, it was the pharmaceutical industry that has been the main beneficiary of the healing properties of the rainforest trees. It is not just the scores of lives that have been saved from malaria because of the bark of the Quinine tree (*Cinchona officialis*); the list is extensive: Curare (*Chondrodendron tomentosum*), used as poison in blow-darts by rainforest hunters, has found applications in anaesthesia; Guaraná (*Paullinia cupana*) is a trendy, popular stimulant, but the University of Cincinnati has also patented an extract from its seeds that helps prevent strokes; the fruit of the Açaí palm (*Euterpe oleracea*) is eaten by athletes because of its high carbohydrate content.

The most celebrated of the indigenous trees, one that allowed the explosive growth of the whole car industry, is the Rubber tree (*Hevea brasiliensis*), one of those plants that can thankfully be industrially farmed. The latex is a white, smelly resin that oozes from the tree when the bark is cut with a blade. It solidifies as it runs down to a collecting bucket in a process called tapping. It was a novelty product used for erasers and laboratory tubes until Charles Goodyear patented a process called vulcanization in 1844. Vulcanized rubber was stable and hard, accepted high loads by stretching, and bounced back into shape when the stress was removed. When the new invention, the automobile, required durable wheels, rubber tyres were the obvious solution.

The ever-expanding demand for rubber created a boomtown in Manaus where the astounding Amazonas Opera House, inaugurated in 1896, is a permanent reminder of the lavish lifestyles of the rubber barons during the late 19th century. The

Amazon fish

monopoly of what became increasingly an essential commodity resulted in the best-known biopiracy case of all time. In 1876, Henry Alexander Wickham – later knighted by King George V – filched rubber tree seeds from the Amazon basin and smuggled them in banana skins to the Royal Gardens at Kew. They ended up in plantations in the British colonies in Southeast Asia, which today is the source of 90% of all natural rubber worldwide.

This episode left deep marks in the Brazilian psyche and stringent biopiracy laws have been enacted. In compensation – and to attract foreign know-how and capital – the Brazilian federal government is providing economic initiatives to attract foreign biotechnology partners to Manaus for joint research into the commercial exploration of rainforest organisms.

Amazon fish

Most of the beautiful, appealing fish that dwell in household aquariums such as Angel fish (*Pterophyllum sp.*), Discus fish (*Symphysodon sp.*), Headstander (*Anostomus anostomus*), Corydora catfish (*Corydoras sp.*) and cichlids like the Oscar fish (*Astronotus ocellatus*) or the Blue Acara (*Aequidens pulcher*), stem from the 2000-plus species that are found in the Amazon. In the river's impenetrable muddy waters a bright colour or striking pattern is the only way to attract mates or to follow the rest of your shoal.

For those with a frisson for the unusual, the infamous Red Piranha (*Pygocentrus nattereri*) has also become a top aquarium choice, if only because one can come face to face with one of the most fearsome creatures of the river. Its looks match its reputation: large eyes, a bulldog's mouth with sharp teeth that protrude upwards and a blood-red belly give it a fierce, brutish appearance. Soon the aquarium enthusiast will discover that piranha behaviour in captivity mimics that in the wild. They prefer low light and foliage to hide behind, both for defensive purposes – they are preyed upon by caimans and dolphins – and to ambush their prey. They will also eat anything that moves in their environment, be it another aquarium species or even a fellow piranha that might be some centimetres smaller.

Above: Latex runs from a rubber tree in a centuries-old technique. Native Indians used it for waterproofing their canoes.

The Amazon Rainforest

Piranhas

Although it is true that a school of piranhas can tear a large animal to shreds within minutes, they are not an aggressive species. They only strike when the animal is dead or bleeding and in distress – witness the rare attacks against humans despite the fact that locals regularly swim in the Amazon's waters. Recent research has also indicated that they shoal not to hunt in packs, but to defend themselves against predators. And yes, they have a taste for flesh, but they are also omnivorous, eating anything from insects to fruit and seeds.

Still, there is one Amazon fish that can make grown men faint. It is the *candiru* or 'Vampire Fish' (*Vandellia cirrhosa*), the smallest catfish known to science, measuring about 1cm (0.3 in) in thickness and up to 15cm (6 in) in length. It is slippery, slender, wormlike and very agile. Its mouth contains razor-sharp teeth that munch their way through flesh. *Candirus* are parasitic and attack a larger fish through its gills. Once inside they use their teeth to bite an artery and gorge themselves on the host's blood. Locals believe that the *candiru* mistakes the urea that is expelled from fish gills for the flow of urine. Being as thin as a maggot, it slides up the engorged urethra and hooks itself in the urinary tract. As it cannot travel back to the water, it is impossible to dislodge and dies, so immediate surgery becomes necessary. Such parasitization on the urinary tracts of humans – both male and female – has often been reported but usually dismissed. However, one attack on a male urinating in the Amazon was recently documented and the resulting surgery videotaped. It appears that, rare or not, such attacks do happen.

The one fish whose reputation is fully deserved is the Electric Eel (*Electrophorus electricus*), which is not a true eel but a brown-orange elongated freshwater fish that can reach 2.5m (8ft) in length and 20kg (44 lb) in weight. Although it has gills, it obtains around 80% of its oxygen from the air and needs to come up to the surface every 15 minutes to breathe through its mouth. This feature allows it to live in the low-oxygen muddy bottoms of the lower and middle Amazon.

Most of its vital organs are in the front 20% of its body and the rest contains its electric organs – the Sachs and Hunter electroplaques that are stacked like disks in a battery and can deliver a 600V jolt, which it uses for both hunting and defensive purposes. These organs develop soon after birth, with fry even as small as 15mm (0.6 in) using a weak electric field for orientation. This allows it to swim around their parents who will protect their nest and their spawn aggressively.

The eel's body has a potential difference, with the head having a positive charge and the tail a negative charge. The pulse is created by sending small positive sodium ions through a channel in its body, momentarily reversing the polarity and creating electricity.

Aquatic mammals

It uses both Sachs and Hunter organs to hunt: as it is almost blind, its Sachs' organ produces weak 10V pulses to locate other small fish. Since it lacks sharp teeth to hold on to any prey that is trying to escape, it then uses its stronger Hunter's organ to stun its victim, which is then sucked into the mouth of the eel.

Aquatic mammals

One of the most peculiar-looking animals you are likely to find in Brazil is the *peixe-boi* or Amazonian Ox Manatee (*Trichechus inunguis*), a large, grey, shiny-skinned aquatic animal that looks like a hippo, but swims like a seal. Its two nostrils are at the top of its snout, its front limbs, whose lack of nails have given it its scientific name (*inunguis*), have evolved into flippers, whereas its rounded rear has no legs and is employed like a gigantic paddle. It is the smallest member of the order *sirenia*, named as such because the animals were sometimes mistaken for, or gave rise to the myth of, sirens and mermaids. Well, sailors used to spend very long periods at sea.

Below: Swimming with manatees is offered to visitors by many eco-lodges.

The Amazon Rainforest

Adult manatees reach a length of about 2–2.5m (6–8ft) and weigh around 200kg (441 lb). They are preyed upon by jaguars and caimans but their main enemy is man. Locals still hunt or farm them in tanks for their meat and fat. They are totally vegetarian and their constant grazing underwater grinds their molars, so new teeth emerge from the back of their mouths to replace worn teeth at the front throughout their life. This is a characteristic that they share with the land mammals they are closest to, the elephants.

During the rainy season manatees feed in the backwaters and lagoons of seasonally flooded *igapó* forest. That is when a single calf is born; it forms a strong bond with its mother who feeds it from a single teat below the flipper and takes care of it until it is three years old. Manatees can consume up to 8% of their body weight in one day to store fat for the dry season when they return to the deep rivers. The deposits of fat and a slow metabolism ensure their survival during the dry season when they may not feed for weeks or months.

Manatees are tame and curious and will readily swim with you like dolphins, should you want to take a dip in the river with them. Oddly, the locals shy away from the real Amazon dolphins, the *botos*, or Pink River Dolphins (*Inia geoffrensis*); it is widely believed that they are malignant spirits and that they attack humans. According to folk tradition, *botos* can change into handsome, dapper men with hats that cover their blowholes who wait by the river banks to woo and waylay beautiful maidens; conveniently, they are blamed for out-of-wedlock pregnancies.

It is easy to see why *botos* appear creepily anthropomorphic to the natives. They have no fins on their back, but instead display a ridge, like the spine of a muscular youth. Their pink, almost human-coloured bodies are long and chubby and they seem to paddle with their fins. They are almost blind, since sight is useless in the murky waters of the rivers, and they use sonar to wend their way through the flooded forest. Their foreheads are round and protruding like an old man's, their snouts thin and elongated, and their necks flexible enough to turn in all directions. Finally, unlike their sea cousins, they are solitary, slow swimmers and will shadow boats and pirogues even into shallow waters.

Aquatic mammals

This behaviour may have added to their being associated with bad spirits which is why they have never been hunted. Despite this, they are now classified as vulnerable, because they are accidentally killed as fishing bycatch, via collisions with motor boats and through habitat degradation. They are not prolific breeders: the female may give birth to only five or six calves throughout her life.

The *boto* is not the only river dolphin: there is a second species, the *tucuxi* (*Sotalia fluviatilis*). Since it resembles the bottlenose dolphin, swims in shoals and keeps to deep water, it has acquired the opposite reputation to the *boto*: it is considered a sacred animal that brings drowned people back to the shore. Locals respect the *tucuxis* and don't hunt them, so their numbers are stable – although they are subject to the same accidental depopulation as the *botos*.

Birds Translated

English name	Brazilian name	Scientific name
Black Skimmer	Talha-mar	*Rynchops niger*
Brazilian Cormorant	Biguá	*Phalacrocorax brasilianus*
Capped Heron	Garça-real	*Pilherodius pileatus*
Guianan Cock-of-the-rock	Galo-da-serra	*Rupicola rupicola*
Golden Conure	Ararajuba	*Guaruba guaruba*
Harpy Eagle	Gavião real	*Harpia harpyja*
Hoatzin	Jacu-Cigano	*Opisthocomus hoazin*
Large-billed Tern	Trinta-réis-grande	*Phaetusa simplex*
Little Blue Heron	Garça-azul	*Egretta caerulea*
Long-billed Woodcreeper	Arapaçu-de-bico-comprido	*Nasica longirostris*
Musician Wren	Uirapuru-verdadeiro	*Cyphorhinus aradus*
Red-billed Toucan	Tucano-assobiador	*Ramphastos tucanus*
Red-breasted Blackbird	Polícia-inglesa	*Leistes militaris*
Screaming Piha	Biscateiro	*Lipaugus vociferans*
Thrush-like Wren	Garrinchão	*Campylorhynchus turdinus*
Toco Toucan	Tucanuçu	*Ramphastos toco*
Tui Parakeet	Tuim	*Brotogeris sanctithomae*
Turquoise Tanager	Saíra-de-bando	*Tangara mexicana*
White-throated Kingbird	Suiriri-de-garganta-branca	*Tyrannus albogularis*

THE CERRADO

Brazil's low-lying bush country of the central state of Goiás provides some of the best opportunities to view wildlife. In the extreme northeast lies the Parque Nacional da Chapada dos Veadeiros, easily reached by State Highway GO-118. Diametrically opposite on the border with Mato Grosso do Sul and located 800km (497 miles) west of Brasília is the Parque Nacional das Emas. Both parks were jointly inscribed as UNESCO Natural World Heritage Sites in 2001 and their biological significance cannot be underestimated: they contain 60% of all floral species and 80% of all vertebrate species of the Cerrado. As the inscription citation itself says, because of their location in the central plateau of South America, they have acted as ecological sanctuaries to various species escaping from climate instability over the millennia, including the present climatic changes. Nothing could prove the point more dramatically than the sighting inside the Parque Nacional das Emas in 2003 of the Cone-billed Tanager (*Conothraupis mesoleuca*), thought to be extinct since 1938.

Animal, Bird and Plant Life

The Cerrado biodiversity hotspot contains:
160 species of mammals
150 species of amphibians
120 species of reptiles
837 species of birds
about 1000 species of trees and shrubs
about 3000 species of herbaceous plants

Opposite top to bottom: *Vale da Lua, a rocky valley; an adult margay; landscape at Parque Nacional das Emas:* Campo Limpo *with termite mounds.*

The Cerrado

Parque Nacional das Emas

Park Statistics

Area: 1318km² (508 sq miles).
Rainfall: The annual precipitation is 1500–1700mm (59–67 in) with three months (June–August) totally dry. The wettest months are December–March.
Temperature: The average is 22–24°C with a low of 8°C (46°F) in June and a high of around 30–31°C (86–88°F) in January/February.
Opening Times: 08:00–18:00 Tue–Sun. No admittance after 12:00. Entry is R$3 per person. During October and November, guides will keep the park open for visitors well after sunset to observe the bioluminescence phenomenon.

The Emas National Park lies on the plateau (350–1000m/1148–3281ft high) that separates three big Brazilian hydrographical basins: the Plata in the South, the Amazon in the north and the Pantanal swamplands in the west. The vegetation consists of tall Cerrado trees (5–6m/16–19ft high) plus transitional altitudinal vegetation between the Cerrado and the lowlands. *Campo limpo* grasslands made up of dart grass (*Erianthus agustifolius*) occupy 60% of the park's area and patches of *mata ciliar* composed of Buriti palms (*Mauritia flexuosa*) are conspicuous by the banks of the Rio Formoso and Rio Jacuba. There are excellent examples of *campo sujo* where grass coexists with Rhea's Fruit trees (*Parinari obtusifolia*), Cashews (*Anacardium occidentalis*) and Copaíbas (*Copaifera officinalis*).

Although the park is famous for its rheas (*emas*) and for the highest concentration of Red-and-green Macaws outside Amazônia, it is teeming with other wildlife. In a survey undertaken in 2000, 500 bird, 78 mammal, 84 reptile, 21 amphibian and 12 fish species were recorded. All five species of armadillos in Brazil live here; macaws, curassows, toucans, giant anteaters, tegu lizards, boa constrictors and anacondas are frequently seen. Finally, 11 jaguars and 33 pumas have been counted and are being monitored in the section called Furnas, which is criss-crossed by streams and creeks.

Right: A Buff-necked Ibis or Curicaca (*Theristicus caudatus*) in the Parque Nacional das Emas.

Parque Nacional das Emas

If you drive on the dirt roads of the park in the late afternoon, you will probably scare off some corpulent birds that fly off with some effort and a lot of noise. You may falsely identify them as partridges and this is what the locals call them: *perdiz*. They are, in fact, tinamous, one of the most ancient order of birds around, whose fossil record goes back 10 million years. There are 47 species living in South America, but the one you will more likely have encountered is the Red-winged Tinamou (*Rhynchotus rufescens*).

Best time to go
The dry season is between April and October. After July the drought causes animals to search for food during the day. On the other hand, the beginning of the rain period in October coincides with the phenomenon of termite nest bioluminescence.

How to get there
The Emas National Park can be entered via two gates. The easiest access is via Mineiros, 435km (270 miles) from Goiânia via Federal Highways BR-060 and BR-364 and then Federal Highway BR-359 for another 91km (56 miles) to the northern Jacuba gate.

The Guarda da Bandeira gate is in the south where the park headquarters are also situated. It is accessed via the GO-302 unpaved road 27km (17 miles) from the small village of Chapadão do Céu, 594km (369 miles) from Goiânia. The village is itself reached via a well-signed turn off from the BR-364, but this involves driving 121km (75 miles) on an unpaved road. There is no accommodation and no food in the park. Only access with a registered IBAMA guide is allowed and numbers are limited on various trails to 10 per guide. There is one bus a day from Goiânia to Mineiros which takes six to seven hours. Once there, you can easily find guides from the *Prefeitura*.

Bioluminescence
There is no better time to be in the Emas National Park than after dusk on a hot night in October at the onset of the rainy season. It is then that the 2.5 million-odd termite mounds that fill the expanse of the plateau sparkle with aquamarine fairy lights in a unique display of bioluminescence.

Accommodation

The base for most visits to the park is the city of **Mineiros** (population: 40,000) where there are many restaurants, bars and a range of hotels.

Pilões Palace: The best option, also signposted from the main avenue. Praça José Alves de Assis, tel: (64) 3661-1547. Recommended.

Hotel Dallas: Signposted from the main avenue. 5 Avenida, 223, tel: (64) 3661-1534.

Hotel Mendonça, Rua 9, 94, tel: (64) 3661-1552.

Closer to the park is the smaller and sleepier settlement of **Chapadão do Céu** (population: 5000).

Hotel Vitor, Rua Ipê, 213 Leste – Qd. 1 Lt 12, tel: (64) 3634-1722.

Pousada das Emas, Rua Ipê, Qd. 17 Lt 1, tel: (64) 3634-1382.

The Cerrado

Bird Life

Whistling Heron
Southern Lapwing

Birds of prey:
Crested Caracara
American Kestrel
Burrowing Owl
White-tailed Hawk
White-tailed Kit

Threatened species:
Black-masked Finch
White-winged Nightjar
Dwarf Tinamou
Yellow-faced Amazon
Rufous-sided Pygmy-tyrant
Lesser Nothura
Brazilian Merganser

Bioluminescence is the emission of light by living organisms generated in cells called *photocytes*. These cells burn certain organic compounds called *luciferins* that emit visible light. The best-known luminescent species are fireflies, which use their sparkling light for courtship, but other species use it to attract prey. This is also the purpose of the bioluminescence of the termite mounds of the Cerrado, but it is not the termites that are responsible. Their mounds provide shelter for armadillos, birds, snakes and a unique species of click beetle (*Pyrearinus termitilluminans*) that hatch in their hundreds on the mounds around October, because it is then that termites grow wings to fly off and build more colonies. The luminous radiance from the beetles' abdominal lanterns attracts the flying termites that seek out the light, only to be devoured as they pass by the hungry beetle larvae.

Rhea

The rhea – along with the penguin and the Patagonian Propeller Duck – is one of the three flightless birds of South America. The Greater Rhea (*Rhea americana*) belongs to the ratite family like the ostriches of Africa. It should not be confused with another ratite, the emu of Australia, despite being called *ema* in Portuguese. And yes, the Greater Rhea's abundant presence has named the Emas National Park.

Rheas' wings are no good for flying, but help the birds keep balance and change direction when running at speed. Their powerful legs and broad, three-toed feet can propel them to speeds in excess of 60km (37 miles) an hour, enabling them to out-run most predators.

The rhea is omnivorous and will eat leaves, fruit, seeds, insects, even small animals like rodents and lizards. It is smaller than an ostrich and with a less flamboyant grey, pale-brown plumage. It is the continent's largest bird, with an adult male reaching 1.7m (5.5ft) height and a weight of 35kg (77 lb). Unlike the pair-forming ostriches, however, the rhea's reproductive behaviour is vastly different. A male has a harem of between two and 12 females and, after mating with them, he builds a nest on the ground where each female lays her eggs in turn; she can lay many, weighing 500–700g (18–25oz) each. It is then the male who

Parque Nacional das Emas

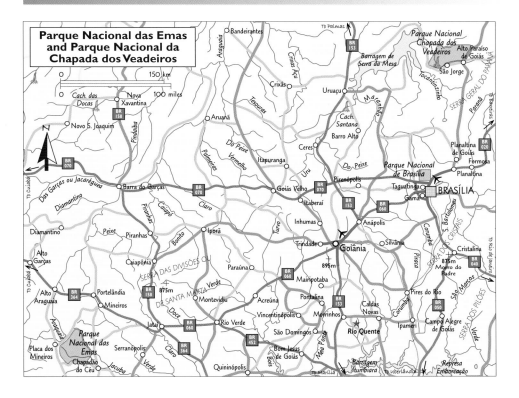

Parque Nacional das Emas
and Parque Nacional da
Chapada dos Veadeiros

incubates them for about 40 days, while the females leave to
attach themselves to another harem. During rearing, the male is
extremely aggressive and will attack anyone and anything that
approaches his chicks, even predators and humans.

Where to go

There are many trails through the park adding up to 400km (248
miles) undertaken by car and on foot. If you want to see the
whole park you should allow about three days, depending on how
much time you want to spend on foot.

Park traverse

It is possible to cross the park by car from north to south in one
day (51km/32 miles) starting at one of the gates of the park and
ending in the other. In about the middle of that road, there is a small

The Cerrado

walking trail to the best panoramic vista of the park, the Mirante do Avoador, with a view towards the valleys of the Furnas carved by the various creeks and their confluence with the Rio Jacuba. This is where the big cats such as jaguars and pumas roam.

If your drive is from north to south you will pass through many kilometres of *campo sujo*. When you reach the grasslands of *campo limpo* and the termite mounds, look out for several fire breakers – land that has been deliberately scorched either side of the road to stop any advancing fires during July to September.

Southern circuits
If you start from the Porta da Bandeira, take the left road towards Glória in the extreme southwest, before you reach the park HQ. After about 4km (2 miles) passing through open grassland, you will find the small Glória stream and groves of Buriti palms in an example of *mata ciliar*. This is a place where soldiers were stationed during the Paraguayan War (1864–70) and old pieces of ammunition are still being found in the

Below: The landscape of Campo Sujo on highway BR-359 from Mineiros to Parque Nacional das Emas.

Parque Nacional das Emas

undergrowth. The road goes around in a circuit so keeping to the right will return you to your starting point until you see a sign for Park HQ. Continue to the bridge over the Rio Formoso, where on a clear day you can see the rocks all the way to its bottom 4m (13ft) down and, if you are lucky, you may spot anacondas. Before you return to the gate, take a left to the Lagoa da Capivara to observe capybara and marsh deer. Continuing on will take you via a small unused exit to the road back to Chapadão do Céu.

Northern trails
Starting from the Jacuba gate there is the Jacubinha walking trail and then the new Homem Seco 2.5km (1.5-mile) trail where it is possible to see deer, coatis, capuchin and howler monkeys. Both can be completed within an hour. This is the only area of the park where you can enter *mata da galeria*, closed canopy forest, but take care: during the dry season, the woods harbour the painful *carrapatinhos* ticks, so cover up well and use talcum powder on the exposed parts of your body.

Outside the park
There is plenty to do around the park itself. Fifty kilometres (31 miles) north of Mineiros there are rock formations and river springs in the Pinga Fogo and Forminguinha complexes that create pools of water where it is possible to swim. Eighty-one kilometres (50 miles) south from Chapadão do Céu there is a large complex of sandstone caves at Serranópolis with rock paintings that date back 10,000 years.

Big cats
As in Africa, where everyone wants to see a lion, everyone wants to see a jaguar (*Panthera onca*) in Brazil. Yet this is a wish that is rarely granted, as the top predator in the Neotropics is very elusive, its habits are nocturnal and its spots camouflage it perfectly. Out of all national parks in Brazil, however, Emas is the one where you are most likely to encounter the continent's biggest cat, or at least see its tracks on the ground and hear its roar. Although there are only 11 jaguars within the confines of the park, during the dry period they have been known to hunt during the day as well as at night.

Cerrado Medicinal Plants

Many plants of the Cerrado have strong medicinal properties that are only now being fully evaluated; a recent study has counted 509 medicinal species belonging to 297 genera and 96 families. Some have been used in local traditional medicine for centuries and can be bought locally. Some examples:
The bark extract of **Barbatimão** (*Stryphnodendron adstringens*) has antifungal properties and is used against thrush.
The bark extract of **Pau-terra** (*Qualea grandiflora*) is used against gastric ulcers.
The root extract from **Amica** (*Lychnophora ericoides*) is used to treat wounds, pain and inflammation.
The oil of the seeds of **Fava-de-santo-inácio** (*Pterodon pubescens*) is used for its anti-rheumatic activity.
Tea from the leaves of **Catuaba** (*Anemopaegma arvense*) is sold as a natural aphrodisiac.

The Cerrado

Endangered Animal Life in Emas National Park

Excepting the giant otter, all of Brazil's endangered **large mammals** can be found here:

Jaguar
Maned Wolf
Bush Dog
Giant Anteater
Giant Armadillo
Marsh Deer
Pampas Deer

On the smaller end of the spectrum:

Woolly Giant Rat
Pygmy Short-tailed Opossum

Morphologically, the jaguar is most closely related to the leopard but it is much bigger and more brawny. It is as long as a grown man (around 180cm/71 in without its tail) and it can reach the weight of a lioness (150kg/330 lb). It can live for over 24 years in captivity, more than other feline species. It stalks and kills with a powerful leap-and-bite and to this end it has developed a most formidable sets of jaws, penetrating even an armadillo's armour. It kills its prey – anything from marsh deer and tapirs to monkeys and caimans – by biting through its brain, breaking the skull in the process. Strangely – and some say mystically even – it abandons the area where it has killed for a long period afterwards to move somewhere else; for this reason the effective catchment area of the jaguar is something like 100km^2 (39 sq miles).

The jaguar, along with the tiger, the puma and the ocelot, is a cat species that actually swims readily, and it lives near rivers and lakes, stalking its prey as it comes to drink. It even jumps into the water to kill its prey – typically a capybara – and is strong enough to drag it back to the shore. Although rarely, it does attack humans but they mostly survive, which means that such attacks are usually defensive.

Jaguars are solitary and the male and female separate immediately after mating, which can happen throughout the year. After a gestation of 90–100 days the female gives birth to a litter of up to four cubs that are blind for their first two weeks. The mother is very protective of her young, and does not allow any males to come close, as they sometimes devour them.

The mythology surrounding the jaguar is extensive, as it has always been a local symbol of power and majesty. Representations of the animal have been found in Mayan temples in Yucatán and on Moche ceramics in Peru. For the Xavante people who live in the lower reaches of the Amazon basin, the jaguar has divine qualities. Originally friendly, it was the keeper of fire until man stole a hot coal from its hearth with the help of the other animals of the forest. It is this transgression that caused the animal's fury and its resulting transformation into the ultimate jungle avenger.

Big cats

The jaguar is endangered due to loss of habitat and is protected in Brazil, although ranchers will kill any encroaching animal that threatens their herds. Trade in its pelts, as for all big cats, is absolutely forbidden.

The puma, cougar or mountain lion (*Puma concolor*) is the other big carnivorous feline found in Brazil and is, in fact, after man, the mammal with the largest distribution range in the New World, found from the Yukon to Patagonia. The puma and the jaguar are both called *onça* in Portuguese and the locals refer to both uniformly, differentiating between them as *onça pintada* for the jaguar and *onça parda* for the puma, only if you ask.

A male puma is smaller than the jaguar, reaching 2m (6.5ft) in length for males (of which 70–90cm/28–35 in are its tail) and can weigh up to 120kg (264 lb); females are just over half the size of the males. Both sexes have a coarse pelt with a uniform brown-yellow upper coloration. Their throats and chests are white and their noses are

Below: Jaguars are highly territorial animals and will fight off any intruder.

The Cerrado

pink with a black edging. The adults are solitary and only come in contact during mating. This can happen at any time of the year and is instigated by the female who growls loudly when she is in heat that lasts up to nine days. Males establish their territory which is generally twice as large as the jaguars' and they demarcate it with urine scent; they won't attempt to mate until they have created such a home area, a fact that may explain their wide dispersal in the Americas. They allow females to have their own intersecting ranges, but expect to have preferential copulation rights. A female will give birth after a gestation of around 90 days to a litter averaging two to three cubs and will care for her young that are born deaf and blind (and remain so for ten days) for about one year.

Like jaguars, pumas stalk and ambush their prey, biting or breaking their necks. They do attack humans with an increasing frequency as other prey becomes scarce, urban population encroaches in their territory and they become more and more habituated to humans. In the United States there have been 50 attacks since 1991, with a dozen cases reported just in California; two-thirds of the fatalities are children. These should, however, be kept in perspective: it is rarer to die of a puma attack than from a poisonous snake bite.

Below: Early puma lore is full of stories of how the animals loved and protected humans. Recent attacks are a reversal of such behaviour.

Smaller cats

Brazil's forests also harbour populations of ocelots (*Leopardus pardalis*), animals similar to jaguars but easy to differentiate because they are only about twice the size of a domestic cat. Their markings also tend to be more striped around the head and neck. Normally nocturnal, they do occasionally hunt during the day, which is why any feline tracks in the parks are likely to belong to an ocelot. They are keen swimmers, quite adept in catching fish. They only hunt smaller animals and are themselves preyed upon by jaguars. Because they are easier to catch, they have been hunted in large numbers for their pelts, the mainstay of the fur trade, and are highly endangered. Apart from living in pairs, their reproductive behaviour is similar to that of the jaguars.

Looking very much like an ocelot, but with a longer tail and as small as a domestic cat, the margay (*Leopardus wiedii*) is another rare denizen of Brazil. Strangely, DNA testing has established that, like the ocelot, it has only 36 chromosomes as opposed to 38 for all other cats. It is mostly arboreal, using its long tail as a ballast like a monkey. Its party trick is unmistakeable: its hind ankle joint rotates a full 180 degrees, allowing it, unlike most other cats, to run down a tree head first. As it is the only feline that does not breed in captivity, it is now being phased out from zoos and attempts are being made to stabilize its numbers in its natural environment. It usually only gives birth to a single kitten, a fact which has sadly contributed to its low numbers.

The wild cat you are most likely to encounter is the jaguarundi (*Herpailurus yaguarondi*) that hunts during the day. You may not recognize it as a cat, however, because it resembles a big fat weasel. It stands 40–60cm (16–24 in) high, reaches a length of 60–70cm (24–27 in) without its tail and weighs up to 6kg (13 lb). Its coat is sleek and unmarked, its tail is flat like an otter's and its ears are small and rounded. They can be domesticated; Amazonian tribes keep them as pets to control rodents around their encampments, much like Old World populations did with domestic cats. As they have never been hunted for their unremarkable pelt, they are not endangered.

Cerrado Fruit

The Cerrado has many endemic, characteristically sweet fruit that are not found elsewhere, the most common ones being:

pequi (*Caryocar brasiliense*)
– also used to make a local liqueur
mangabá (*Hancornia speciosa*)
araticum (*Annona crassiflora*)
cagaita (*Eugenia dysenterica*)

All are easily and cheaply available in local markets.

The Cerrado

Park Statistics

Area: 655km² (253 sq miles).
Rainfall: 1500–1750mm (59–69 in)
Temperature: 24–26°C (75–79°F)
with a maximum of 40–42°C
(104–107°F) and a minimum
of 4–8°C (39–46°F).
Opening Times: R$3 per entrance
08:00–12:00; park gate open
until 18:00. Closed Mondays.
During school holidays (January,
February and July) the park is open
every day. No children under five
years allowed. There is a daily limit
of 200 persons on the Canyon trail
and 250 persons on the Waterfalls
trail accompanied by an IBAMA-
certified guide.

Parque Nacional da Chapada dos Veadeiros

The combination of accessibility, mysticism and a glorious primeval landscape makes the Chapada dos Veadeiros ('Deerhunters' Flat') one of the most visited parks in Brazil. At 1800m (5904ft) in altitude, at lies in the highest point of the *Planalto Central* and, with its several waterfalls and canyons, mountain peaks and beautiful valleys, highlands and lowlands, it is considered a paradise by canyoning, abseiling and rock-climbing enthusiasts as well as by nature watchers. The contours in the park are the oldest in South America, having been created some 1.8 billion years ago by immense tectonic compression forces, responsible for its extensive quartzite seams.

The park contains 1000 species of plants, 500 of trees, 160 mammals, 300-plus birds, 60 reptiles and amphibians, 49 species of fish, and it is one of the last refuges of the South American maned wolf.

The park also contains the dramatic waterfalls of Rio Preto that are 100m (328ft) high, two deep forested canyons, spectacular mesa shapes and therapeutic springs. The occasional unexpected reflection of light from a crystal that emerges from the ground flanked by beautiful orchids during a walk in the park makes it easy to see why many believe that it is the centre of convergence of cosmic energy. This is a park that is marketed heavily inside Brazil and it has a healthy number of visitors from within the country, but outside the peak periods of December–February and July you will find it quiet.

Best time to go
During the dry season: May–September. Hikes to Canyons 1 and 2 are closed at the height of the rainy season.

How to get there
The Chapada of the Veadeiros National Park of the is off the highway GO-118, 260km (161 miles) north of Brasília.

It can be reached by regular buses that leave from the main Brasília bus station towards the village of Alto Paraíso de Goiás. From there, one bus a day goes to the small village of São Jorge, 36km (22 miles) away, at the edge of the park.

Parque Nacional da Chapada dos Veadeiros

If travelling by car, leave Brasília on BR-020, towards Formosa Goiás. After Planaltina, take a left on Highway GO-118 which will take you to Alto Paraíso. The national park lies 36km (22 miles) from the town on the unasphalted GO-327 by the village of São Jorge. The road is bad and it takes one hour to drive between the two villages.

Where to go
Inside the park
Only two trails are open to the public inside the park. The Canyons trail is the easier of the two and leads to Canyons 1 and 2 and the waterfall known as Cariocas (10km/6 miles return). The Waterfalls trail (9km/5 mile return) is of medium difficulty and leads to the Rio Preto Falls 1 and 2 (80m/262ft and 120m/ 393ft) – one wonders who named these sights so imaginatively.

The vegetation includes riverbank palm forests (*mata ciliar*), high-altitude Cerrado as well as open (*vereda*) and closed gallery forest (*mata da galeria*), plus sparse, rocky *campo rupestre* patches. Trees to look out for are Ipé trees (*Tabebuia ipe*), Copaibas (*Copaifera sp.*), Buriti palms (*Mauritia sp.*), and Babassu palms (*Orbignya martiana*). There is no shade on the trails and the sun is stronger at the plateau, so wear a hat and apply sun block liberally.

The Waterfalls trail is rocky and slightly descending. It passes by several open holes that were quartz mining sites, in operation until 1961. It takes 30–45 minutes to reach the 120m (394ft) waterfall where there is a panoramic point, and a further 45 minutes to the 80m (262ft) waterfall that forms a small water hole where it is possible to swim. After that there is a testing, steep descent of 800m (2625ft) to the Correideiras of Rio Preto where you can lie down for 'hydromassage' as the rapids between the rocks knead your back. From there is takes about one to two hours to return to the entrance.

The Canyons trail is easier and a little bit more shady, passing through flat scrubland punctuated by small cascades that are good for swimming and, when you stand under them, hydromassage. In order to reach Canyon 1 you must ford the river, which is why the trail is closed when it is raining and the river current is stronger. After that you reach Canyon 2 where the river passes

Accommodation

The main infrastructure is in the small village of **Alto Paraíso de Goiás**, but **São Jorge** has the advantage of being next to the park entrance (for accommodation, see next page).

Pousada São Bento: 10km (6 miles) from Alto Paraíso, 8km (5 miles) of dirt road by the Rio dos Couros. Two local attractions, the waterfalls of São Bento and Almécegas, are at the back of the hotel, tel: (62) 3459 3000, www.pousadasaobento.com.br

Camelot Inn: The main building looks like a castle and the chalets have a medieval ambience. No aircon, fans instead. There is a restaurant inside the hotel. Km 168 on GO-118, 100m (104yd) outside the entrance to Alto Paraíso, tel: (62) 3446-1449, www.pousadacamelot.com.br Recommended.

Pousada dos Anões: This is a private reserve of 18,000m^2 (193,680 sq ft) with its own forest, hikes, caves and waterfalls. Km 144 on GO 118, tel: (62) 3459-3434, www.pousadadosanoes.com.br

Recanto da Grande Paz: Rua João Bernardes Rabelo 112, tel: (62) 3446-1452, www.recantodagrandepaz.com.br

Portal da Chapada: 11km (7 miles) from São Jorge towards Alto Paraíso, tel: (62) 9669-2604, www.portaldachapada.com.br

The Cerrado

Accommodation in São Jorge

Pousada Casa das Flores:
Minimum two days. Rua 10 quadro 2,
lot 14, tel: (61) 3455-1055,
www.pousadacasadasflores.com.br
Pousada Aldeia da Lua: 8km (5
miles) on the road to Alto Paraíso,
tel: (61) 9602-6456,
www.aldeiadalua.com.br
Ecopousada Cristal da Terra:
Chalets and apartments with
hammocks around a central pool.
Rua 1 quadro 3, lot 1,
tel: (61) 9978-9128,
www.pousadacristaldaterra.com.br
Recommended.

Right: Chapada dos Veadeiros, trail of the Waterfalls, vista point of Fall 1 of 120m.

through and forms a large pool at the end. It is only 30 minutes to the final stop by the twin Cariocas waterfall but the descent is again tricky.

Outside the park

When the national park was created in 1960, it encompassed a much larger area that included a lot of private land. As the years passed, it shrank, leaving the private land intact. What this means is that there are many walks and points of natural beauty outside the park around the two villages of Alto Paraíso and São Jorge and along the GO-239 that exist near or on private reserves. Those mentioned below are at least as worthwhile as the park itself and every single one has a place to swim.

Parque Nacional da Chapada dos Veadeiros

By the Rio Couro there is a small dirt road that leads to the **Cataratas do Couro** – four waterfalls of 150m (492ft) each. Access is by 4WD over 19km (12 miles) of paved road and 31km (19 miles) dirt road from GO-118 towards Brasília at the turn-off by the Fazenda Boa Esperança.

Almécegas is a single waterfall 50m (164ft) high and 30m (98ft) wide that can be reached at a turn-off 10km (6 miles) on the GO-239 by Portal da Chapada.

There are two main vista points to stop on the GO-239 on the way west to São Jorge: on Km 21 the **Morro da Baleia** (1500m/4922ft), a huge quartzite rock that can be climbed to provide views over the park, and the **Morro do Buracão** (1576m/5171ft), a much more difficult proposition on Km 20.

But by far the best excursion is from the village of São Jorge on a wonderful 4.5km (3-mile) trail to the **Vale da Lua**, a rocky valley (containing grottoes and water holes) which was eroded 600 million years ago by the Rio São Miguel. The last 1.8km (1.1-mile) stretch is on private land where entry is R$5 (open 08:00–17:00). You can also reach the entrance by car, but the walk from São Jorge is as good as any of the park's two trails.

New Age mysticism

As the Chapada's crystals are supposed to concentrate energy, New Age mystics from all over the world have been congregating in nearby villages to absorb the cosmic power that is allegedly emanating from its quartzite seams. During the 1980s the community of Alto Paraíso de Goiás became a centre of spiritualists, healers and believers in a mixture of Western and Oriental beliefs, which explains the many outlandish structures in the village. It lies near the 'sacred' 14th parallel – signposted from the village – which also passes through Machu Picchu, supposedly another centre of cosmic energy and proof of extraterrestrial visitation. According to psychics, the sheer quantity of quartz crystals present in the soil of the park makes it one of the most luminous regions seen from space – a fact unconfirmed by NASA.

Bird Life

Some common birds are:
Helmeted Manakin
Purple-throated Euphonia
Rufous-tailed Jacamar
Hepatic Tanager
Macaws
Toucans
King and black vultures

Animal Life

Pampas Deer
Swamp Deer
Jaguars
Armadillos
Giant Anteaters
Capybaras
Tapirs

The Cerrado

The area between the Chapada and Brasília has one of the highest number of UFO sightings in the world outside the United States. Two main cults are also based in the region: the 5000-strong settlement of Temple of Dawn near Planaltina, a mixture of Scientology, Egyptology and millenarianism, and the Church of Goodwill which is headquartered in Brasília and whose main temple is a seven-fold pyramid with one of Chapada's large quartz crystals at the top. Not to be outdone, Alto Paraíso contains a replica of Stonehenge – except that the monoliths are no taller than an average man.

Maned Wolf

The Maned Wolf, *Chrysocyon brachyurus*, is an animal only remotely related to the wolf and domestic dog. With 78 chromosomes instead of 76 for all other canines, it is the only member of a separate genus, *Chrysocyon*. Its Latin name reflects its striking rusty-red coloration which, along with its long, slender legs, justifies its nickname, 'fox-on-stilts'. Its mane is composed of erectile hairs that are raised whenever the wolf is threatened in order to make it look more physically aggressive. As big as an Irish wolfhound, the adult stands about 1m (3ft) tall at the shoulder and weighs 20–25kg (44–55 lb). It uses its strong-smelling urine with its distinctive sulphur odour to demarcate its territory – averaging 25km² (9 sq miles) – and to mark its hunting trails. One of its distinctive hunting features is stomping on the ground to wheedle out prey from holes.

Along with many large South American mammals, maned wolves are not strictly carnivorous. Only half of their diet consists of rodents, armadillos, birds and reptiles; the other half consists mainly of plant material, with an overwhelming preference for one particular green, tomato-looking fruit, *Solanum lycocarpum*,

Above: A maned wolf. *Its long, slender legs are an evolutionary response to the grasslands of the Cerrado where it roams.*

Maned Wolf

which, in Brazil, is called *lobeira* or 'wolf's fruit'. You can find many inside the Chapada itself.

Unlike their gregarious cousins, maned wolves are solitary, nocturnal and reclusive. They are monogamous and a couple share their territory. Mating takes place from November to February and, after a gestation of 75 days, the female gives birth to a litter of two to six pups, each weighing about 450g (16oz). The maned wolf is an endangered animal, mainly due to loss of habitat and because it has been hunted for the magical quality of its body parts: its eyes are powerful good luck charms; canines are worn around the neck to protect someone from dental problems; and eating its internal organs supposedly saves a snake-bite victim from death. To top it all, maned wolves are subject to imported canine diseases like distemper, toxoplasmosis, intestinal parasites and even rabies.

Birds Translated

English name	Brazilian name	Scientific name
American Kestrel	Quiriquiri	*Falco sparverius*
Black-capped Antwren	Chororozinho-de-chapéu-preto	*Herpsilochmus atricapillus*
Coal-crested Finch	Mineirinho	*Charitospiza eucosma*
Curl-crested Jay	Grallha-do-campo	*Cyanocorax cristatellus*
Helmeted Manakin	Soldadinho	*Antilophia galeata*
Hepatic Tanager	Sanhaçu-de-fogo	*Piranga flava*
Large-billed Antwren	Chorozinho-de-asa-vermelha	*Herpsilochmus longirostris*
Masked Tanager	Saíra-mascarada	*Tangara nigrocincta*
Pale-crested Woodpecker	Pica-pau-louro	*Celeus lugubris*
Purple-throated Euphonia	Vem-vem	*Euphonia chlorotica*
Red-legged Seriema	Seriema	*Cariama cristata*
Red-winged Tinamou	Perdiz	*Rhynchotus rufescens*
Rufous-tailed Jacamar	Bico-de-agulha-de-rabo-vermelho	*Galbula ruficauda*
Scaly-headed Parrot	Maitaca	*Pionus maximiliani*
Southern Lapwing	Quero-quero	*Vanellus chilensis*
Whistling Heron	Maria-Faceira	*Syrigma sibilatrix*
White-banded Tanager	Cigarra-do-campo	*Neothraupis fasciata*
White-rumped Tanager	Bandoleta	*Cypsnagra hirundinacea*

LITORAL:
FERNANDO DE NORONHA

The archipelago of Fernando de Noronha, 345km (214 miles) northeast of Cabo de São Roque on the mainland of Brazil and three degrees below the Equator, is literally without par. This is not just because of the exceptional submarine coral landscapes: there simply are very few tropical islands in the South Atlantic. The Fernando de Noronha islands are the remaining peaks of a volcanic mountain ridge submerged 12 million years ago, with the most recent activity around 1.5 million years ago. The waters plunge very quickly down to 4000m (13,124ft) below sea level, creating a current that brings up nutrients from below. As a result, the islands have become an oasis of marine life and are important ecological bases for the breeding and feeding of tuna, sharks, sea birds, turtles and marine mammals.

In 1988, approximately 70% of the archipelago was declared a marine park, with the northwestern part of the main Noronha island populated by 2200 permanent residents that live off tourism. It was subsequently inscribed as a UNESCO World Heritage Site in 2001.

Animal Life

The Fernando de Noronha archipelago is home to the largest number of tropical seabirds to be found in the Western Atlantic; it also is the main breeding ground for the rare hawksbill turtle. It has the only oceanic mangrove forest in the South Atlantic with an area of 1500m² (16,140 sq ft). To top it all, it has the highest occurrence of resident dolphins anywhere in the world, with one species, the Rotador or Spinner Dolphin (*Stenella longirostris*), coming to breed in the waters of the Baía dos Golfinhos (Dolphin Bay).

Opposite, top to bottom:
A rare hawksbill turtle; the Red-billed Tropicbird; the Atlantic Masked Booby with one of its chicks.

Litoral: Fernando de Noronha

Park Statistics

Area: 11.2km² (4 sq miles) of which 85% is in the sea and 15% on the land corresponding to approximately 65% of the island area, the smallest of Brazil's national parks.
Rainfall: It varies from about 180mm (7 in) per month in the dry season to 2700mm (106 in) in the wet, with an annual average of 1250–1500mm (49–59 in)
Temperature: The climate is tropical with a wet and dry season but the temperature remains standard around 25–32°C (77–89°F) all year with an average of 26–27°C (79–80°F).
Opening Times: The marine park is clearly always open, but visits are limited by boat times. There is an eco-tax for anyone visiting the archipelago of around R$33 per person per night (exact amount adjusted annually for inflation) for the first week and progressively less the longer you stay.
Note: Noronha is one hour ahead of Rio/São Paulo.

Opposite: A tegu or tejú lizard. Introduced in the Noronha archipelago, it has now become a pest.

Fernando de Noronha Marine National Park
Best time to go
The dry season is between August and January. However, the wet season (February to July) is best for surfing. High season is July and December–February when prices double.

How to get there
By air from Recife or Natal (daily, about 90 minutes' flight time).

Flora and Fauna on Fernando de Noronha
The main island used to be forested, but it was cleared in the mid-20th century when it was used as a concentration camp for political prisoners. The present secondary vegetation resembles that of the *agreste* in the nearest mainland, the state of Pernambuco. The semi-deciduous trees that lose their foliage in the dry season can reach heights of 15m (49ft), such as an endemic fig tree, the Gameleira (*Ficus noronhae*). There is also the Mulungu (*Erythrina auranthiaca*) – also called 'coral tree' because its flowers are the colour of red-orange coral – whose bark is used traditionally as a sedative. Notable shrub-like plants are the Wild Bean (*Capparis cynophallophora*) and the Burra-Leteira (*Sapium sceleratum*), a spurge species whose sap irritates the skin worse than poison ivy.

There are four main species of bird that live and breed on the archipelago: the endemic Noronha Vireo (*Vireo gracilirostris*) and the Noronha Elaenia or *cocoruta* (*Elaenia ridleyana*), plus two immigrants, the Eared Dove (*Zenaida auriculata noronha*) and the Cattle Egret (*Bubulcus ibis*). The Noronha Vireo is a curious and vivacious green-brown bird that approaches humans without fear, and has the odd habit of foraging for insects while hanging upside down from branches. It is abundant in the forests of the island and resembles a European Reed Warbler but with a longer, sharper bill.

Depending on the time of year, other migratory species come to breed in the archipelago: the Red-billed (*Phaethon aethereus*) and White-tailed Tropicbirds (*Phaethon lepturus*), the Masked (*Sula dactylatra*), Red-footed (*Sula sula*) and Brown Boobies (*Sula leucogaster*), the Magnificent Frigatebird (*Fregata magnificens*), the Sooty (*Sterna fuscata*) and White Terns (*Gygis alba*), the latter a pure white bird that lays its eggs expertly in the elbows of branches, and finally the Brown (*Anous stolidus*) and Black Noddies (*Anous minutus*) that build algae nests in the trees and on the cliffs of Noronha. Sea turtles such as the Hawksbill Turtle (*Eritmochelys imbricata*) and the Green Turtle (*Chelonia mydas*) also visit the islands to lay eggs on a few beaches that are off limits during the breeding season.

Apart from a very large rat (*Noronhomys vespuccii*), now extinct, discovered by Amérigo Vespucci when he moored on Noronha in 1503, no other mammals used to live on the islands. Many of the animals you see today have been introduced by man and some have predictably caused havoc with the wildlife. European rats came first, uninvited, and bred quickly in the absence of predators, so the Tegu Lizard (*Tupinambis merianae*) was introduced from the mainland in the 1970s to prey on them. The lizard, however, found feeding on birds' eggs much easier than running after svelte rats, and devastated the avian population.

There are no snakes on the islands (and the only dangerous animal is a species of scorpion). There are two unique native lizards instead. The first is the Noronha Worm-lizard (*Amphisbaena ridleyi*) that lacks legs, looks like a snake and feeds only on snails; it can be easily seen on the slopes of rocky

Visitor Restrictions

There is a small airstrip for flights from Natal and Recife, about two dozen restaurants, a dozen bars, two supermarkets, an Internet café, plus several diving, sailing and sightseeing companies. Occasionally, a cruise ship stops by at the new modern pier in the port of Santo Antônio. The number of tourists is strictly controlled in a programme that has up to now combined successfully a modest tourist infrastructure along with the preservation of the delicate marine ecosystem. Visitor numbers are restricted to 420 per day and the level of accommodation on the island to a maximum of 1000 beds. However, paradise does not come cheap: room rates are in line with those of Ipanema and Copacabana for even the most basic *pousadas*. The service does not always match the prices: for instance, there is no draft beer, and coffee is of the powdered soluble type. Embratur classifies the lodgings on Noronha as one, two or three 'dolphins'. For a list of accommodation options, *see* panels, pages 60 and 61.

Litoral: Fernando de Noronha

3 dolphins
Pousada Maravilha: Simply stunning location, modern (since 2003) with jet-setting clientele. On the BR-363 (Sueste), tel: (81) 3619-0028, www.pousadamaravilha.com.br
Zé Maria: Ecologically sustainable, with a view of the Morro do Pico. Rua Nice cardeiro 1, Floresta Velha, tel: (81) 3619-1258, www.pousadazemaria.com.br
Pousada Solar dos Ventos: One of the long-standing *pousadas* of the island, on the BR-363 (Sueste,) with a view of the Bay of Sueste, tel: (81) 3619-1347, www.pousadasolardosventos. com.br/pousada.html
Pousada da Morena: Free Internet. Rua Nice Cordeiro, 2600 Floresta Velha, tel: (81) 3619-1142, www.noronha.com.br/ morena/index.htm

formations such as the Morro do Pico. The second is the Noronha Skink (*Euprepis atlanticus*) whose population is being reduced because of competition with introduced animals such as the Tegu lizard. Rather puzzlingly, DNA analysis of the Noronha Skink shows that its provenance is from Africa rather than South America. During periods of drought, when water is scarce, both endemic lizards climb up the flowering Mulungu trees to drink the nectar of the flowers in an example of ecological specialization.

What to see
The islands
The 21 islands of the archipelago have 545km (338 miles) of coastline and contain no fewer than 16 beaches where water visibility can be as deep as 40m (131ft). The main island, Noronha, contains 90% of the total area and is an undulating plateau at an elevation of 60m (197ft) with cliffs along the south, sandy beaches and dunes in the north and west, an extensive mangrove forest in the southeast, and several small springs and streams during the rainy season.

In the early morning various boats leave from the pier of Santo Antônio for various tours. The ruins of the 17th-century Portuguese fort of Remédios are near the start of the shortest Federal Highway in Brazil, the BR-363. The islands visited in the 'Inland Sea', north of Santo Antônio, are: Ratos, the second largest island situated at the most northern point, followed south by the islands of Meio, Sela Gineta, Rasa, São José, Cuscus and Fora. Landing on any of the islands is not permitted.

The beaches
Below Santo Antônio, there is a stretch of paradisiacal beaches with sugar-white sand and thick tropical vegetation. In increasing order of distance from the main town, they are: the small inlet of Praia do Cachorro just below the village of Remédios which leads gently to the Praia do Meio, the beach normally used by the locals. It contains the Pedra do Pião, a huge rock balanced very precariously that has stood there since time immemorial. Over the next cliff – and Portuguese fort – the large Praia da Conceição offers a startling glimpse of the highest point of the island, the rocky thumb-like 323m (1060ft) Morro do Pico, one of the local landmarks.

Fernando de Noronha Marine National Park

Beyond, there is the Praia do Baldró, a surfers' beach and the first of a continuous stretch of *praias*, starting with Dos Americanos – named after an old US guided missile and satellite tracking station. The next one down is Praia do Bode, reached via a rock-strewn path, and the Cacimba do Padre which contains the most haunting of ruins, the Citadel of São Batista de Dois Irmãos. One of the few springs of the island is located nearby and every passer-by has a sip; legend has it that those who drink from its waters will return to Noronha. A trail leads from Cacimba do Padre to the Dois Irmãos (Twin Cliffs) and into the Praia dos Porcos. This is a stony, rocky seascape with reefs full of surface fissures that create pools where sea life is trapped at low tide and where the multicoloured reef fishes can be seen close by as if in artificial fish tanks. Snorkelling is allowed at sea, but not in those fragile reef pools.

Next comes one of the two most popular and secluded beaches: the Praia do Sancho, which is voted year-in, year-out as one of the most beautiful beaches in Brazil. It is secluded, charming, with crystal-clear waters and fine gold sands. Its access is via a set of steps on a steep sandstone cliff. There is a remarkable vista point northwards to the Dois Irmãos as a trail leads you to the Mirante dos Golfinhos further south.

The final bay on the northern side of Noronha island is the famous Baía dos Golfinhos (Dolphin Bay) which has been called 'the world's largest aquarium'. There are few trees, no beach, and the cliffs that rise sharply are mostly populated by the Roadside Woodrose, or Jitirana (*Merremia cissoides*), an introduced climber that was brought in for cattle feed and ended up as a pest, strangling native vegetation. The bay has the calmest and deepest waters on the islands but is out-of-bounds and demarcated by buoys in order not to disturb the 350-odd spinner dolphins that frequent it on a daily basis. Their antics, including their mating displays and sea-jumps, can be seen from a vista point, the Mirante dos Golfinhos (Dolphin Belvedere). Usually, one can see them playing and jumping to a depth of 55m (180ft) below sea level and up to 500m (1640ft) away.

Accommodation Options (cont.)

2 dolphins
Pousada Beco De Noronha:
Rua das Acácias, Floresta Nova,
tel: (81) 3619-1568/1569,
www.becodenoronha.com.br
Pousada Mabuya: Rua Major
Costa 124, Trinta,
tel: (81) 3619-1205,
www.mabuya.com.br
Pousada Maratlântico:
Qd M Lt 6, Floresta Nova,
tel: (81) 3619-1915/2281,
www.pousadamaratlantico.com.br

1 dolphin
**Pousada Algas Marinhas Alameda
das Flores:** 118, Floresta Nova,
tel: (81) 3619-1341,
www.pousadaalgasmarinhas.com.br
**Pousada Colina Dos Ventos
Estrada da Colina:** 6 Vila do Trinta,
Tel: (81) 3619-1257/1738,
www.pousadacolinadosventos.com.br
Pousada das Flores: Rua Dom
Juquinha, 111, Vila do Trinta,
tel: (81) 3619-1224/1870
www.noronhaflores.com.br

Litoral: Fernando de Noronha

The Hawksbill Turtle

The hawksbill turtle is a species that has been hunted almost to extinction because it provides the main commercial source of tortoiseshell. Its beautiful red-and-amber streaked carapace has been used to manufacture anything from ornaments and combs to glass frames and guitar plectrums. An international hunting ban in 1973 couldn't come too soon, as 80% of the hawksbill population disappeared during the 20th century. Unfortunately, substantial illegal black market trade went on until at least the 1990s, when international bodies redoubled their conservation efforts. Given that the turtles take several decades to mature and that the females lay their clutches every two years, these beautiful reptiles are still a threatened species.

The Capim Açu-Farol trek

The main island trail is the 4.8km (3-mile) Capim Açu-Farol trek that must be undertaken with a guide and runs through the body of the island. The grade is hard in the first 800m (2625ft) because the track climbs up very steeply over sharp volcanic rock, but for the most part it's easy. It passes through all the geological zones of the island and provides an excellent introduction to its vegetation in the best-preserved part. There are 360-degree views in all directions and, during low tide, it is possible to walk a 2.8km (2-mile) extension that ends in the enchanting Praia do Leão in the eastern, more protected, part of the island. This is a copy-cat version of Praia do Sancho, and serves as a turtle sanctuary. During certain parts of the year the sea turtles come to lay eggs and the beach is closed between 18:00 and 08:00. The main rock in the bay, named the Little Widow (*Viuvinha*), is a breeding ground for sea birds.

South and East

On the southeastern side of the island is the Bay of Sueste, whose calm, tranquil waters are the feeding grounds of sea turtles. It also serves as an alternative mooring point on the island if the rip tides in the north pier are too strong. The left-hand side of the beach and of the bay itself are out of bounds, demarcated by buoys, but one can bathe and snorkel on the right-hand side with a high probability of swimming among sea turtles in their natural habitat. It is here that the only Atlantic island mangrove forest exists, which again is off limits.

One of the wonders of the archipelago is the coralline algae reef on Atalaia Beach – one of the few in the world – which is composed of 'false coral' corallimorphs. The algae that make up the reef are milky-pink and are extremely sensitive to pollution. For this reason, guided tours of only 100 people per day are allowed, 20 at a time, at low tide, with a maximum of three hours to be spent on the beach. The wearing of fins and, more importantly, sun block is strictly forbidden.

Diving

The island is home to several diving companies that have a range of programmes from beginners' courses to providing assistance and equipment to certified divers. The dive sites around the island

Noronha dolphins

include several shipwrecks (including an old, sunken Portuguese frigate), underwater caverns, paleovolcanic formations and encounters with reef fish of every colour in the spectrum, plus the usual dolphins, sharks and sea turtles.

Noronha dolphins

The Spinner Dolphin (*Stenella longirostris*) is the most eye-catching denizen of the Noronha archipelago. Up to 2m (6ft) long and weighing 75kg (165lb), it has a grey-black back, white belly and silver fins. It is called 'spinner' because of its tendency to jump out of water and rotate several times around its axis. Its movements seem to be related to its daily activities such as feeding, state of alert and calls to the pod to regroup. It is thought that the aerial assaults are timed to perfection so that specific waves and vibrations are generated as a dolphin hits the water, allowing it to communicate with its peers.

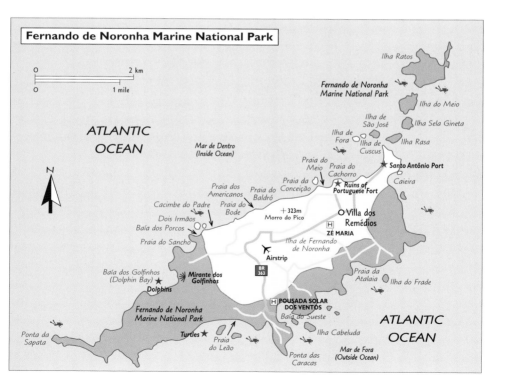

Fernando de Noronha Marine National Park

2 km
1 mile

ATLANTIC OCEAN

N

Ilha Ratos

Fernando de Noronha Marine National Park

Ilha do Meio

Ilha de São José
Ilha Sela Gineta

Ilha de Fora
Ilha de Cuscus
Ilha Rasa

Mar de Dentro (Inside Ocean)

Praia do Meio
Praia do Cachorro
Santo Antônio Port

Praia da Conceição
Ruins of Portuguese Fort
Caieira

Praia dos Americanos
Praia do Baldró

Cacimbe do Padre
Praia do Bode
+323m
Morro do Pico
O Villa dos Remédios

Dois Irmãos
ZÉ MARIA

Baía dos Porcos

Praia do Sancho
Ilha de Fernando de Noronha

Airstrip

Baía dos Golfinhos (Dolphin Bay)
Mirante dos Golfinhos
BR 363
Praia da Atalaia
Ilha do Frade

Dolphins

Fernando de Noronha Marine National Park
POUSADA SOLAR DOS VENTOS
Baía do Sueste

ATLANTIC OCEAN

Ponta da Sapata
Turtles
Praia do Leão
Ilha Cabeluda

Ponta das Caracas
Mar de Fora (Outside Ocean)

Litoral: Fernando de Noronha

Dolphin Biology

As with all deep-sea mammals, dolphins' biology is insufficiently known, and one of the main global centres of research is the Projeto Golfinho Rotador, here on Fernando de Noronha. Its aims are to study the animals' behaviour, preserve their environment and promote a programme of environmental consciousness for the locals. One of its findings was the interconnectedness of the ecosystem: faeces and partly digested excreta of spinner dolphins function as a regular food supply to at least 12 species of coral reef fish that would normally be expected to feed on algae and plankton. Six per cent of dolphins are also in symbiotic relationships with Whalesuckers (*Remora australis*), small open-water fish up to 50cm (19 in) that are normally attached to large cetaceans, feeding off spilled prey and fungus that lives on their skin.

The spinner dolphin swims in the tropics throughout the globe and is the third most common dolphin species. It can move in a catchment area of 700km^2 (270 sq miles) and cover a distance of 150km (93 miles) in a day. A school moves about with a speed of 5–10km/h (3–6 miles/h) but individuals have been timed racing up to 40km/h (24 miles/h). Being a pelagic mammal, it hardly ever comes close to the continental shelf, so it tends to congregate on oceanic archipelagos, with two main hot spots: Kealakekua Bay in Hawaii and Dolphin Bay in Noronha.

Spinners are gregarious and form matriarchal family groups led by the oldest female. However, they may be joined by others so that pods of up to 1200 individuals can form spontaneously and loosely. Male adults assume the rotating position of 'security guards' and organize parties to attack or escape from sharks. It is those security guards that come close to the tourist boats; they are in reality trying to divert the boats' attention from their friends and family.

The daily circle of their activities on the island consists of nocturnal feeding – they are so active that they can eat up to 5% of their own weight per day – and returning to Baía dos Golfinhos at sunrise. During their daily rest the dolphins enter a stage of lower metabolism equivalent to 'alpha' sleep in humans; they also bob up and down between the surface and the bottom of the bay in a rhythmic pattern. At sunset there is a general exit back to their feeding grounds and the cycle starts again.

The best time to see their spins and turns is when they enter the bay between 06:00–07:00. At that time, volunteers from the Projeto Golfinho Rotador are on hand to explain the dolphins' behaviour to visitors.

Spinner dolphins are polygamous, promiscuous and, like humans, their sexual behaviour seems not always to have a reproductive end. The gestation period is about 10 months and the newly born babies are just 75cm (29 in) long. Suckling is frequently observed in the bay, when the calf stands on its side and places its snout alternating from one teat to the other, in order to drink its mother's extremely fatty milk.

Noronha dolphins

The interdependence extends to mutual help with other dolphins, for spinners are not the only ones to grace the waters of the Noronha archipelago. Smaller populations of Painted Dolphins (*Stenella attenuata*), identified by their sharply demarcated beak, spotted body and downward-curving fins, also live in the park. Their lives are complementary to the spinners; they feed through the day and come to rest at Baía dos Golfinhos during the night when the spinners leave. This association is beneficial to both, because it means that someone is always on alert against sharks.

The only time when the dolphins seem stressed is whenever Humpback Whales (*Megaptera novaeangliae*) appear around the island between July and November, especially when they approach the Baía dos Golfinhos. Along with Melon-headed (*Peponocephala electra*) and Pilot Whales (*Globicephala sp.*), humpbacks visit the island on the way to the Abrolhos archipelago further south where they reproduce.

Above: Pods of five to six male spinner dolphins are sizeable enough to fight off larger predators such as tiger sharks.

Birds Translated

English name	Brazilian name	Scientific name
Cattle Egret	Garça-vaqueira	*Bubulcus ibis*
Eared Dove	Arribaçã	*Zenaida auriculata noronha*
Noronha Elenia	Cocoruta	*Elaenia ridleyana*
Noronha Vireo	Sebito	*Vireo gracilirostris*

CAATINGA

The Caatinga is one of the last semi-arid areas in the world with a significant degree of biodiversity, sheltering little-studied flora and fauna: out of 615 species of plants in the Caatinga, 443 are endemic, as well as 19 out of its 140 species of mammals. Although vegetation is dominated by drought-resistant succulents and thorny trees, this transition zone between the Cerrado and the Mata Atlântica is not an outright desert. Its many microclimates within eroded canyons and river beds provide unexpected surprises, such as groves of introduced Mango trees (*Mangifera indica*) and the indigenous shrubby Juazeiro tree (*Ziziphus joazeiro*) whose bark infusion is used as an antipyretic and whose fruit is fermented into wine by the locals.

Animal Life

Ocelot
Margay
Crab-eating Fox
Lesser Anteater
Armadillo
Black Howler Monkey
Rock Cavy
Fruit-eating Bat

Opposite, top to bottom:
Two Red-and-green Macaws sitting in a tree; a nine-banded armadillo; two ocelots playing in the trees.

Caatinga

Park Statistics

Area: 922km² (356 sq miles) (reduced from 980km²/378 sq miles).
Rainfall: 0–990mm (0–39 in) with an average of 500–750mm (20–29 in) annually, but any rain falls between October and March and in the big drought of 1983 it didn't rain for another three years.
Temperature: The annual average temperature is 24–26°C (75–79°F) but it varies tremendously. During the hottest period of the year between October and December, the average is 35°C (95°F) with the highest recorded being 47°C (116°F). In June, temperatures can drop down to 8–10°C (46–50°F).
Opening Times: 08:00–17:00. $3 entrance fee. Walks allowed with a registered IBAMA guide only.

Parque Nacional da Serra da Capivara

The Serra da Capivara National Park – the only national park representative of the Caatinga – is located in the southeast of the state of Piauí, right in the middle of the Brazilian backlands, the *sertão*. It is rated as the most interesting of all national parks by Brazilians themselves: apart from being physically spectacular – cliffs sculpted by rain erosion rise up 270m (886ft) on the horizon for 180km (112 miles) to form the Northeastern Massif – it also is one of the most important prehistoric archaeological sites in the world.

Best time to go

In autumn and early winter, from March to July.

How to get there

The park is difficult to get to and is situated very far from the two nearest cities: Teresina, the state capital, is 530km (329 miles) away and Petrolina, the nearest big city, is 311km (193 miles) away in Bahia. Both cities have airports. The main infrastructure is provided in the villages of São Raimundo Nonato (population: 28,000) 41km (25 miles) away and, to a lesser extent, Coronel José Dias (population: 4000).

From Petrolina: Take the BA-235 highway from Petrolina in Pernambuco until you reach Remanso in Bahia and then change to BR-324 into Piauí to São Raimundo.

From Teresina: Take the BR-343 to 6km (4 miles) beyond Floriano, then turn to the PI-140 (that becomes BR324) to São Raimundo. There are daily buses to São Raimundo from both cities.

What to see

There are 14 park trails of varying difficulty that should be visited by car or on foot as early in the day as possible, before the sun starts baking in the afternoon. They lead to geological formations, rock paintings, vegetation examples and wildlife viewing. Certain trails were actually marked by the prehistoric inhabitants of the area and are some of the most ancient walkways known to anthropologists. The Visitors' Centre in the park has maps and arranges guided walks.

Parque Nacional da Serra da Capivara

Pedra Furada – Canoas – Rodrigues-Meio circuit

This is a one-day, medium-difficulty circuit that starts from the Visitors' Centre, which has a small café, toilets, a permanent exhibition hall, an auditorium with video shows, a souvenir shop and picnic areas. It passes by more than 10 important sites, including the *Boqueirão* (small river duct) of Pedra Furada. It is there, among the many paintings that span a wall area of 70m x 8m (230ft x 26ft), that lie in the most controversial of findings in the park: signs of a human-made fire that has been carbon-dated to 50,000 years ago. The trail passes several small caves, some of which provided archaeologists with pottery that can be seen in the Museum of American Man in São Raimundo (*see* panel, page 77). Some of the most exceptional sites are in the Toca do

Accommodation

All in São Raimundo Nonato:

Serra da Capivara: On highway PI-140, 2km (1 mile) after the exit towards Teresina. Tel: (89) 3582-1389/1760.

Pousada Real: Largo Manoel Agostinho De Castro, 704. Tel: (89) 3582-1495.

Pousada Lelinha: R. Dr. Barroso, 249. Tel: (89) 3582-2993.

Camping: Pedra Furada at Avenida Nestor Paes Landim Km 28, Sitio do Mocó. Tel: (89) 582-1100.

Caatinga

Rock Art

Serra da Capivara contains the largest concentration of rock paintings and carvings in the Americas, estimated to have been the product of the earliest hunter-gatherers to have colonized the area. There are at present over 300 archaeological sites with 657 rock paintings in shelters carved in rock, the rest being remnants of encampments or villages, fragments of pottery, funeral sites or skeletons of humans and animals such as sabre-toothed tigers and giant sloths. It was the carbon-dating of these sites in 1981 that pushed the traditionally accepted date of human settlement in the Americas to 50,000 years ago. This is a proposition that is still controversial, challenging as it does the traditional view that humans crossed the Bering bridge to the American continent 13–15,000 years ago. The paintings themselves, with scenes depicting war-fighting, hunting, farming, dancing and sexual practices, are more recent, with the oldest panels around 12,000 years old and the majority between 10,000 and 4000 years old.

Funda and the three Fumaça pits where men are presented hunting, and animal figures, such as a jaguar and a row of rheas, predominate.

After these, a descent to the bottom of the valley via the Canoas Circuit passes by paintings depicting humans, capybaras and rheas. Climbing up again, using an iron staircase, you reach the Rodrigues circuit with its grottoes I and II and paintings that are 18,000 years old.

Not far from Rodrigues is the Meio site – human habitation has been detected as far as 14,300 years ago with the remnants of a prehistoric oven, used to cook manioc flour. Ceramic fragments have been dated to 8900 years ago and a polished stone used as an axe dated to 9200 years ago which makes it the earliest human tool excavated in the New World.

Capivara ravine

This is a 43km (27-mile) narrow canyon path straddling high cliffs. It was used for thousands of years by the local tribes; the BR-020 passes through part of it. The rock paintings are typical of the 'Nordeste' period (ca 12,000–8000 BC) and represent scenes from the life and culture of the prehistoric inhabitants, the classic one being humans resting around a tree.

The entry to the path is at the north of the village of Coronel José Dias. It contains the Pit of the Entrada do Baixão da Vaca with a startling 133m (436ft) long wall with 749 painted figures. They belong to the earliest Nordeste period characterized by the movement of the figures. What still amazes the onlooker is that the figures have been clearly designed with perspective. Typically, they are painted with red iron oxide and white clay, although there is one picture at the top of the left side with yellow pigment.

The entry to the Pit of Pajaú contains even earlier rock paintings, with scenes from ceremonies and general rural scenes, the highlights being the graceful 'Three Dancers' and the 'Hunters Using Nets' – a method which is still used by Indian tribes to capture deer today.

Parque Nacional da Serra da Capivara

The Pit of Paraguaio follows on two levels. On the lower level there are paintings of anthropomorphic rheas and deer drawn with such detail that one can distinguish the three species represented (*galheiro, catingueiro* or *campeiro*). On the upper level two graves have been found whose skeletons have been dated to be 8600 and 7000 years old. The earlier one was buried in a round funerary urn in a foetal position and the other like modern man in a square urn with the arms along his sides and the head resting on a stone. The paintings here, being abstract and geometric, are completely different from those in the rest of the park.

If possible, try to include the medium-difficulty, two-hour Veadinhos Azuis circuit whose major 'wow' factor is the only known use of blue pigment on prehistoric rock paintings – until recently when another site was found in Colombia.

Baixão das Mulheres

This 25km (15-mile) easy trail goes through a canyon with 60m (197ft) high walls. It starts from Pedra Furada and passes by the Baixão das Mulheres I that was discovered only in 1973 and contains some remarkable paintings. The most striking one is of a large bird with its wings open, a figure that is part of all New World indigenous cultures and known in North America as Thunderbird. The Baixão das Mulheres II was discovered even later after subsidence caused by a flash flood. The style here is more recent, dated to 8000 years ago. Further in, at the Clovis pit, there is another unique painting – a jaguar designed with open flowing lines that looks more like a Khoi-San painting from South Africa.

Trail of Perna and Andorinhas

An easy trail starts by the western entrance at Terra (or Serra) Vermelha on Km 17 of PI-140 and proceeds to the Baixão da Barriguda circuit (about 6km/4 miles). This is one of the most picturesque trails, notable for its relatively dense vegetation, and it is also one of the best places to see wildlife in the Caatinga, passing by several water holes where animals congregate.

From there, you reach the Perna circuit with its graphic depiction of sexual acts, including what seems to be a scene of group sex in

The Boi Waterhole Circuit

This is an easy 8km (5-mile) circuit that reaches a permanent underground reservoir which overflows into a river during the rainy season. Here live fish, still unstudied, that are endemic to this particular water hole and have evolved in isolation for longer than 10,000 years. There is ample vegetation around with shady trees, tall grass and ferns.

Bird Life

Broad-tipped Hermit
Red-and-green Macaws
Blue-fronted Amazon
Cactus Parakeet

Caatinga

Right: A lesser anteater feeds on an anthill. By the time soldier ants have congregated, the anteater will have moved on.

Plant Life

Ocoteas (*Ocotea fasciculata*)
Eymas (*Pouteria reticulata*)

Cacti:
Xique-xique (*Pilosocereus gounellei*)
Mandacaru (*Cereus jamacaru*)
Quipá (*Opuntia inamoena*)

the Chico Coelho pit. The paintings are concentrated mostly in the Baixão do Perna I, one of the sites of the park whose walls have crumbled because of rain and humidity. It was originally excavated between 1980 to 1989, and remnants of hundreds of fires were found inside, as well as stone tools and bones of consumed animals dated to between 10,000 and 3000 years ago.

The Baixão do Perna II contains some of the most perplexing paintings of the park – their meaning has not yet been deciphered. In one depiction, a group of people pass between them a small baby figure – it is either a ceremony of sorts or the telling of a myth or historical event.

If you return to the western entrance in the late afternoon you can see *andorinhas* (swallows) arriving to spend the night in a cave.

The anteaters

There are two main species of anteater – *tamanduá* in Portuguese – and you can easily distinguish between them: one is the size of a kitten and the other larger than a Labrador.

The smaller one, the Lesser Anteater (*Tamandua tetradactyla*), is a survivor, more so than its larger cousin. This small mammal, weighing just 9kg (20 lb) and up to 85cm (33 in) long with a prehensile tail that's half as long as its body, is happy to colonize any ecosystem, from the dry, desert areas of the Caatinga to the rainforests of the Amazon and the sharp alternation of dry and wet seasons of the Cerrado. Its size and agility has also helped it survive predators better than its giant relative. It even has man on its side: Amazon Indians keep lesser anteaters as pets to keep their villages free of termites.

It is a solitary animal except during mating; the female gives birth to a single baby in the spring after a gestation period of 130 to 150 days. She suckles it for six months and carries it on her tail for up to a year, depositing it occasionally for safety on a branch while she is looking for food. The lesser anteater spends half of its time foraging in trees where it can hide more easily and only half of its time on the ground. It has an elongated snout with a small opening for its tongue and cream-brown fur with black markings around the shoulders and rump like a vest.

It moves very slowly on the ground and is easily tracked and cornered. However big the aggressor, the plucky little anteater will grab a branch with its tail or steady itself by standing on its hind legs against a tree and opening its front limbs wide, ready to fight. Despite its cute, comical appearance it is anything but: locals claim that it can kill small dogs. As its scientific name implies, it has four sharply clawed digits on its forefeet; they are so sharp that it has to protect even itself from being hurt. Like its giant cousin, it folds its claws against its palms when moving about as it walks on its knuckles.

Giant Anteaters (*Myrmecophaga tridactyla*) are one of Nature's tireless wanderers, spending their whole day looking for ants and termite nests. They can devour up to 30,000 ants a day and, when

Serra da Capivara

The Serra da Capivara was inscribed in 1991 by UNESCO as a World Heritage Site, but its maintenance was abandoned due to lack of funds for about 10 years, during which it became a no-man's-land. Subsequent slash-and-burn farming, collection of wood for fuel and hunting of protected species within the park by the neighbouring population – some of the poorest in Brazil – overwhelmed the environment. Some species like deer, rheas and anteaters almost disappeared and, because of the lack of predators, termite and wasp numbers soared, while their nests and pupae damaged the archaeological treasures.

In the early years of this century, robust management succeeded in turning around the deterioration. The measures earned a commendation by UNESCO for the joint partners in managing the site: IBAMA and the Foundation of the Museum of American Man. Anyone who now makes the long trip to the Serra da Capivara and expects to find an out-of-the-way neglected corner will be pleasantly surprised: the park has some very developed infrastructure, including a Visitors' Centre and a unique prehistoric museum in the nearest town of São Raimundo Nonato.

Caatinga

Omnivorous Anteaters

Although called anteaters, both species are in reality omnivorous animals and, in captivity, they eat everything from fruit to meat. In fact, their preference is for termites, avoiding insects with a powerful sting such as army or leaf-cutter ants. Both species have small eyes and their vision is poor but they compensate with excellent hearing. But it is their strong sense of smell that helps them locate a termite nest on a tree which they then proceed to destroy with their front limbs. They rip open anthills and termite mounds and stretch their pencil-like tongues, that are coated with a sticky saliva, up to 60cm (23 in) out to lick in the insects that stick like flies to flypaper. To make doubly sure, their tongue has backward-facing spines that prevent any prey from escaping. As they have no teeth, they grind their food with their palate and with ingested gastroliths in their gizzard-like stomachs, like domestic chickens. They eat very fast, flicking their tongues in and out of their snouts up to 150–160 times a minute. By the time any soldier ants or termites have congregated to defend their nest, they have moved on.

Opposite: A three-banded armadillo rolled up into a defensive ball.

they stop, they retire in secluded forest cavities or holes which they dig in the ground. They are normally diurnal except when they live near populated areas where they tend to be more nocturnal. Even though they move on all the time, they are highly territorial within the area they are foraging at any one time and they will fight off other anteaters.

They grow to a length of 2.4m (8ft) long – with their heads, bodies and tails accounting for a third each – and weigh up to 70kg (154 lb). Grey-brown with a diagonal black-and-white stripe across the shoulder, their fur is composed of coarse, matted hair that stands 40cm (16 in) high on their bushy tail. Despite their scientific name (*tridactyla*) they don't have three but five digits on both front and hind legs. The name probably stems from the fact that only the three front digits are armed with scimitar-like sharp claws. Giant anteaters are normally docile and try to run away but when cornered they, too, stand up balancing on their tails. They can become very formidable opponents, giving pumas and jaguars a run for their money, with at least one recorded fatal attack on humans (an 18-year-old girl in an Argentinian zoo).

Their heads are long with little dots for eyes and small, round, monkey-like ears. Their walnut-size brains are very small in relation to their body. Their insect diet is poor in relation to their size, so they maintain a low metabolism, walking in a slow shuffle, sleeping up to 16 hours a day. They seem to be able to control their body temperature that can fall as low as 32°C (90°F). Surprisingly, they can climb trees and are very good swimmers.

After a gestation of six months, females give birth standing up, supported by their tails, to one single young at a time, which spends most of its first year hanging on to the tail of its mother. When it falls off, it emits a high-pitched whine; the only other time a giant anteater makes a sound is during a fight when it hisses and roars loudly, possibly for effect. Habitat destruction is the biggest threat to giant anteaters and they are increasingly being killed in road accidents as man encroaches upon their environment.

Armadillos

Armadillos, like the anteaters and the sloths to which they are related, are a part of the order *Xenarthra* (*Edentates*), one of the few that is exclusive to the New World. They are some of the strangest and most fascinating creatures Nature has created. With their banded, armoured shell, long snout, small mouth, sticky tongue and sharp claws they look positively extraterrestrial. The 20 species are spread from Oklahoma to Patagonia, ranging from the dark-brown Giant Armadillo (*Priodontes giganteus*) which is 1.2m (4ft) long and weighs up to 25kg (55 lb), to the pink Fairy Armadillo (*Chlamyphorus truncatus*) which is only 16cm (6 in) long and weighs a mere 100g (3.5oz). The most common ones in Brazil are the cat-sized Six-banded (*Euphractus sexcinctus*), Three-banded (*Tolypeutes tricinctus*) and Nine-banded Armadillos (*Dasypus Novemcinctus*). This last, scientific name is derived from the Latin name for rabbit, and typifies the bafflement of those early taxonomists.

Armadillos – *tatu* in Portuguese – forage on bugs, beetles, ants and termites and, like anteaters, destroy nests with their front claws eating tens of thousands of insects a day with their long sticky tongues. Their carapace, which feels like hard saddle leather, is made out of bone plates called scutes, separated by a number of moveable bands that identify the species. Their armour is actually

Rock Cavy

The Rock Cavy (*Kerodon rupestris*), popularly called *mocó*, is a relative of the guinea pig, but much larger; an adult can reach up to 40cm (15 in) in length and weigh up to 800g (28oz). It looks like the South African dassie (rock hyrax), but with stronger legs, paws that resemble a cat's and long stiff nails that allow it to climb up trees and rocks with ease. The cavy has lived in this area for at least 30,000 years, since its dried excreta have been found in the various archaeological sites of the park. Like the other mammals of the Caatinga, it has adapted well to the high temperatures and lack of water. It lives in the crevices of rocky outcrops that contain shade and humidity. It forms groups with a dominant male who will defend his territory and his harem against other males. Unlike other rodents, the female does not produce an extensive litter, but after a gestation of 75 days gives birth to a maximum of two babies, in order to make sure it can feed its young properly, since food sources are limited. A herbivore, it lives on leaves, sprouts, seeds, fruits, tree bark, roots and tubers. It has been hunted for its pelt and excellent meat. Despite this, it is extremely docile and will not run away or attack when approached, but will instead emit high-pitched sounds to inform others of the danger.

Armadillo Oddities

Despite their common appearance, the behaviour of each species can be very different. For instance, when threatened, the nine-banded armadillo stands on its hind legs to box any attackers like an anteater, the three-banded armadillo rolls into a ball like a hedgehog, and the Hairy Armadillo (*Chaetophractus Vellerosus*) runs away. The Dwarf Armadillo (*Zaedyus Pichiy*) that lives in southern Patagonia avoids much of the hassle by hibernating in the winter. The oddities do not stop with their appearance. When startled, they can jump up vertically one metre in the air, possibly to scare a predator in the wild. They can inflate their stomachs to float across lakes and rivers, or walk their way through the bottom with their claws, holding their breath for more than six minutes. Like anteaters (and sloths), they have a low metabolism and live in burrows in the ground where they sleep for 16–17 hours a day. They make their bedding from grass and leaves they collect specially – and change it every now and again. Nine-banded armadillos always give birth to identical quadruplets that have all developed from the same egg and shared one placenta. The females can actually delay implantation of a fertilized egg to the uterus for up to two years, which helps during periods of drought.

less aimed at protecting them from predators (nothing can withstand those crushing jaguar jaws) and more from ant attacks and thorny vegetation. Along with the lesser anteaters, they are considered national saviours in the Serra da Capivara, since they eat insects that degrade the rock paintings.

They are the only animal (besides humans) that are susceptible to leprosy. They can even pass it on to humans who either handle them or eat their flesh undercooked, as a cluster of infections in Texas proved back in the 1980s. They are particularly valuable in the study of the disease, because their unusually low body temperature makes the disease more virulent.

Vampire bats

There are 1100 bat species around the world and 164 (15%) are found in Brazil. There are only three species that are hematofagous (feeding on blood) – all limited to Latin America – and out of those three, two feed mostly or only on birds. There is only one species that feeds exclusively on the blood of mammals, and has courted the most publicity: the Common Vampire Bat (*Desmodus rotundus*). They are about the size of a mouse, with an average body length of 5cm (2 in), a wingspan of 20cm (8 in) and a weight of about 30–40g (1–1.4oz).

Their reputation is much exaggerated but not totally ungrounded, as vampire bats are the second major source for the transmission of the rabies virus to humans. The progressive disappearance of their habitat, and urban encroachment in their territories, has led to an increase of bat attacks on humans in the last 10 years and a rise in deaths from rabies, mostly in the northeast of Brazil and the mouth of the Amazon. The vampire bats seem to follow the routes of rivers and it is therefore riverside communities and their cattle that are in the front line.

Like other bats, vampire bats emit low-energy sonar pulses to locate their prey in the dark. Their hearing is excellent and they are able to detect the breathing patterns of their potential victims. They also have a set of infrared sensors on their noses that lead them to bite those areas where blood flows close to the skin. If there is fur or hair, they cut it off first with their

Vampire bats

canines and lower jaw teeth, employing them like a pair of shears, and then use their upper incisors to make a small cut that is only about 8mm (0.3 in) deep. Contrary to popular belief, they don't 'suck': they lick and lap up the blood that flows from their victim using a protein in their saliva – rather cheekily named *draculin* – as an anticoagulant (as a result, the wound can bleed on for up to eight hours). Their bodies are specially adapted to their liquid diet: their tongues are adapted to lapping, their stomachs can distend like balloons and the blood passes through their digestive system to the kidneys very fast so that the non-nutrient plasma can be expelled through urination. Finally, their body and bone structure is such that they can fly off immediately, having consumed half their body weight in blood during a 20-minute session.

Vampire bats are social animals, roosting together in colonies of a few dozen to several hundred animals. Because of their specialized diet, they can die if they do not feed for more than three days, so they help each other by regurgitating blood to those individuals who have returned hungry.

Vampire bats breed all year round. At seven months, their gestation period is very long for their size, and the juveniles need to be weaned from milk to blood over an extraordinarily long period that can be up to nine months, progressively licking blood from the mouth of their mother. The current proximity of cattle so close to their forest habitats has led into an explosion in numbers which may account for the increase in the number of attacks on humans.

Outside the Park: the Museum of American Man

The extraordinary Museum of American Man was inaugurated in 1998 in São Raimundo. It belongs to the Foundation that co-manages the park, performs research, certifies park guides, supports the local community through free education, and sponsors environment-friendly projects. The museum has a geological section discussing the various minerals and morphology of the region, a biological section with fossils of extinct animals, and an archaeological section with findings from the park – but only replicas of the skeletons found in the Paraguaio pit. (Entry R$6, open Tue–Thu 09:00–18:00, Fri 09:00–21:00, Sat–Sun 09:00–18:00. Last admission one hour before closing.)

Birds Translated

English name	Brazilian name	Scientific name
Black Vulture	Urubu-de-cabeça-preta	*Coragyps atratus*
Blue-fronted Amazon	Papagaio-verdadeiro	*Amazona aestiva*
Caatinga or Cactus Parakeet	Aratinga-vaqueira	*Aratinga cactorum*
Red-and-green Macaw	Arara-vermelha	*Ara chloroptera*
Turkey Vulture	Urubu-de-cabeça-vermelha	*Cathartes aura*

THE PANTANAL AND BONITO

In the central-western states of Mato Grosso and Mato Grosso do Sul lies possibly the best-kept secret in Brazil: a waterlogged, swampy equivalent to Africa's game parks and one of the world's major freshwater wetland ecosystems. It is the Pantanal, a vast alluvial plain that occupies 138,183km² (53,338 sq miles) in Brazil – the size of Uruguay. Like the llanos of Venezuela, the Pantanal is a seasonally inundated savanna, encompassing perennial wetlands, lakes, grasslands and forests; it lies in the Plata basin, the second major hydrographic basin of the South American continent, after the Amazon. The clay soil does not absorb much water, so from October to April heavy rains cause the Paraguay River and its associated system (São Lourenço, Cuiabá, Taquari, Miranda, Negro and Aquidauana) to overflow, causing waters to rise 40–50cm (15–19 in) in the higher regions for 2–4 months and complete flooding as high as 3–4m (10–13ft) in the low-lying areas for half of the year. The net result is that, after November, around two-thirds of the Pantanal area is under water which starts ebbing in May.

Palms of the Pantanal

The **Acuri** or **Urucuri palm** (*Attalea phalerata*) is a short 8m (26ft) tree whose leaves provide the major source of thatch in the region.

The **Macauba palm** (*Acrocomia aculeata*) is a medium height 15m (49ft) tree with sharp spines that protrude up to 20cm (8 in) perpendicular to its trunk. Its fruit is the main source of food for parrots and macaws. The **Caranday palm** (*Copernicia alba*) is a 20m (65ft) tree with small, edible fruit that are promptly swallowed up by the fish whenever they drop into the water. Anglers also use them as bait.

The **Buriti** or **Wine palm** (*Mauritia vinifera*) is a thin, tall 25m (82ft) tree whose fruit is fermented to produce a local alcoholic liquor.

Opposite, top to bottom:
An anaconda, Pantanal;
swimming in the waters of Rio
Peixe; Roseate Spoonbills.

The Pantanal and Bonito

Pantanal Statistics

Area: 140,000km²
(54,040 sq miles).
Rainfall: 1100mm (43 in) annually,
concentrated from October
to March.
Temperature: The mean annual
temperature is 25°C (77°F).

Tour Operators

Gil's Pantanal Discovery Tours
have an office in the main bus
stations in Campo Grande and
Corumbá and specializes in the
Southern Pantanal. An experienced
company of repute attracting younger
visitors. Recommended.
Tel: (67) 9994-7774,
www.gilspantanaldiscovery.com.br
Armadillo Tours: Offers 4–5-day
packages to Pantanal and Serra da
Bodoquena (Bonito, Jardim e
Bodoquena) in a selection of
comfortable *fazendas*.
Tel: (67) 3028-3030,
www.armadillotur.com.br
Freeway Tours: Based in São Paulo
and operating since 1983, this operator
offers Pantanal tours in the Caiman
Ecological Refuge that can claim the
patronage of Harrison Ford,
Mr Indiana Jones himself.
Tel: (11) 5088-0999,
www.freeway.tur.br

Pantanal

The accessibility, abundance and diversity of the region's animal life – in particular its avifauna – are astonishing. Although there is a national park in the north, the Parque Nacional do Pantanal Matogrossense, which was included in UNESCO's Heritage Sites in 2000, visitors can visit any part of the biome which is still 92% intact and be rewarded with sightings of animals. Even during the scheduled bus service on the BR-262 highway to Corumbá passengers can frequently spot spectacled caimans lying by the roadside and startled jabiru storks flying away.

The national park itself is difficult and expensive to get to. It can be reached only by boat that has to be hired in Porto Jofre about 245km (152 miles) south of Cuiabá, the capital of Mato Grosso. Even reaching Porto Jofre is an adventure: the last 86km (53 miles) after Poconé contain 122 bridges, some in a state of complete disrepair. As the park has no infrastructure and is often wet even during the dry season, most visitors opt for the more easily reachable private *fazendas* of the Mato Grosso do Sul, arranging a jungle tour from Campo Grande or Corumbá. One advantage of visiting the south is that one can also fit in Bonito, the latest 'in' eco-destination in Brazil.

Inside the Pantanal accommodation is normally provided by tour operators, based in Corumbá and Miranda. Companies arrange for transfers to the region with accommodation that ranges from camps to luxury *fazendas*. A good operator should provide you with water, three cooked meals a day and will take you for jungle walks. Local companies offer the best value for money.

Although visitors will find true wilderness, observers are worried about human impact. The expansion of cattle ranching and sport fishing, the increasing cultivation of soya and sugar cane and the construction of ethanol distilleries that provide 'clean' car fuel from sugar threaten the survival of this unique ecosystem.

Best time to go

The dry season is between May and October, but temperatures can drop down to freezing in July.

Pantanal

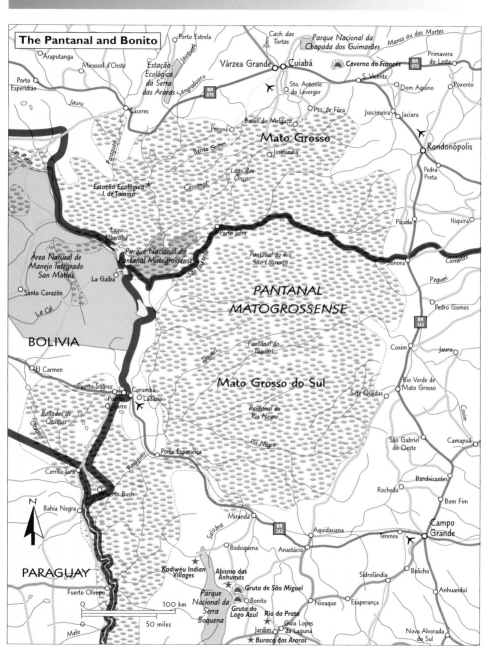

The Pantanal and Bonito

The Pantanal and Bonito

You can arrange tours with private reserves who will come and pick you up from the nearest town:

Ararauna: Luxury resort in the north of the town of Aquidauana, 284km (176 miles) from Campo Grande, where it has an office at Rua Ceará 333. It has a 16m (52ft) high observation tower and offers programmes in conjunction with the Pantanal Institute research centre nearby. Tel: (67) 3348-8191/3348-8190, www.pousadaararauna.com.br

Fazenda Santa Inês: Has an office in Rua Dom Aquino, 542 Campo Grande, and is based 200km (124 miles) away, in Miranda. It organizes horse riding and fishing trips into the Pantanal, including a very interesting boat trip to the Fig Tree Reservation, located by the Rio Salobra. Tel: (67) 9982-9514/4082, www.fazendasantaines.com

Fazenda Baia Grande: Is 24km (15 miles) away from Miranda with activity programs ranging from local rodeo cattle displays, horse riding, walks, fishing, photography tours, two-person canoeing, bird-watching by the Miranda River and others. Tel: (67) 3382-4223/9984-6658/ 9907-3557, www.fazendabaiagrande.com.br

How to get there

The Transpantaneira highway is impassable during the rainy season, so the best way to reach the three main nearby urban areas (Cuiabá in the north, Campo Grande and Corumbá in the south) is by air. The best option is to fly to Campo Grande and continue by bus to Miranda or Corumbá, making a detour to Bonito. You can arrange tours in all these cities.

The Pantanal states of Mato Grosso and Mato Grosso do Sul (where Bonito also lies) are one hour behind Rio/São Paulo.

What to see

Because of periodic flooding there are no trails as such in the Pantanal. Its relatively small size compared to the other biomes renders the landscape homogeneous: low bush and clearings alternate with copses of trees demarcated by lagoons and streams. The big attraction though is not the landscape, but the diverse wildlife that cannot hide behind the dense vegetation of the Amazon rainforest or in the grasslands of the Cerrado.

However, it is the bird life that astounds. This is the main habitat of the proud Jabiru Stork (*Jabiru micteria*), symbol of the Pantanal, as well as large flocks of herons, ibises and ducks. There are 26 species of parrots including the principal remaining population of the world's largest parrot, the Hyacinth Macaw (*Anodorhynchus hyacinthinus*) which is rare everywhere else, except here.

The anaconda

The anaconda (*sucuri* in Portuguese) is the largest species of aquatic, non-poisonous boas. They normally live in the swamps and rivers throughout the South American tropics, although the Yellow Anaconda (*Eunectes notaeus*) can be found as far south as Argentina and is the most common species found in the Pantanal.

But it is the Green Anaconda (*Eunectes murinus*) that has captured the popular imagination. It is considered a terrifyingly colossal snake, but this is mostly due to lore, legend and Hollywood rather than scientific fact: the tale of the *Sucuri Gigante*, the 'giant anaconda', exists in all the tribes of the Amazon – and also among rubber tappers and gold prospectors. One explanation for this persistent

The anaconda

myth was supplied in November 2007 when a stray Minke Whale was found 1800km (1118 miles) inside the Amazon, near the city of Santarém: the locals, who had never seen one, stopped swimming in the river, fearful of 'a giant snake'. This freak incident only needs to occur once per century for a fully fledged legend to appear.

There have also been many exaggerated tales of explorers who have caught sight of 30m (98ft) monsters as thick as a beer barrel – some, unsurprisingly, standing watch over caves with gems and gold – and there have been pictures showing snakes that are so long that they need to be carried by several people in succession. Yet, the hard fact is that in a recent survey of more than 1000 wild anacondas, the largest was around 5.5m (18ft) and weighed 45kg (99 lb).

The green anaconda is not even the longest recorded reptile. The title is still held by a 9.75m (32ft) Reticulated Python (*Python reticulatus*) captured in 1912 in Southeast Asia. Another member of the same species was caught in Indonesia in 2003, supposedly measuring 15.85m (52ft) in length and weighing 447kg (985 lb), but when measured independently the tape could only reach to 7m/23ft. Just to put things into perspective, there exists a $50,000 reward offered by the Wildlife Conservation Society of America for anyone who can capture a snake longer than 9m (30ft). It still lies unclaimed.

The green anaconda is, nevertheless, the most massive reptile on earth, with a girth as big as that of a human adult. It is very aggressive, and there have been reported attacks on Amazon researchers, though thankfully none successful. It is a constrictor, which means that it coils its muscular bulk around its victim and squeezes hard until it suffocates to death (contrary to popular belief, it doesn't crush its bones). It then unhinges its jaw and swallows its meal that can be an animal as large as an adult capybara, a deer, or a peccary. Like all snakes, it has teeth which serve to hold on and gulp down its victim, but its bite is not poisonous. It has a very slow digestive system and, after a meal, it lies along a river bank unable to move.

The green anaconda's bodily colouration is reflected in its name and it has alternating black lozenge spots on its back and ones with yellow centres on its sides. It has a remarkably small head and its nostrils face upwards to allow it to breathe while swimming. It is

Animal Life

Jaguar
Giant Otter
Howler Monkey
Agouti
Armadillo
Lesser Anteater
Tapir
Peccaries
Anaconda
Coati
Spectacled Caiman
Capybara
Crab-eating Fox
Marsh Deer

The Pantanal and Bonito

covered with scales, and the pattern along the underside of its tail is unique to each individual in the same way fingerprints identify a human. It is a sluggish crawler on land, but a very fast and able swimmer in the water which is its proper element.

The female, which is much larger than the male, releases certain specific scents in the air before mating that can attract up to a dozen members of the opposite sex. They all remain coiled together wrestling for days, until she chooses the strongest to copulate with. This is done underwater, as the male wraps his tail around the female and uses spurs that grow around his cloacal area (the cavity where the sexual organs lie) to stimulate the female. When she raises her own cloaca, copulation occurs and the snakes part, although there have been recorded occasions of cannibalism when the female devours her partner. It has been conjectured that this is her last meal before birth, as she will not eat again throughout the six-month gestation. Anacondas are viviparous, which means that the eggs hatch internally giving birth to live young with an average litter of between 20 and 40 juveniles. They grow up quickly but, until they reach a reasonable size, they are heavily preyed upon and very few reach adulthood and sexual maturity.

Below: The jacaré (Caiman yacare) is an adaptive predator with ecological success in every environment.

Caimans

The cry of 'jacaré' is one often heard in the Pantanal, and the first animal a visitor is likely to see is the one the shouting guide is pointing at: the ubiquitous caiman. Endangered it is not: there are anything from 100–200,000 individuals in the region. It wasn't always so; like all crocodilians, it used to be hunted for its skin, and during the 1980s it became a threatened species. The present explosion in numbers is due to the success of subsequent programmes in sustainable farming: current Brazilian regulations require that all

Caimans

caiman skins be produced on breeding farms, be tagged and have a minimum belly width of 18cm (7 in).

Its geographical spread is large – from the Caribbean to northern Argentina – but it is in the Pantanal that it features as one of the main attractions. Surprisingly for such a plentiful animal the scientific classification of caimans is still a subject of debate. The current consensus is that there are four main species: the Black Caiman that lives mostly in the Amazon (*Melanosuchus niger*), the Broad-snouted Caiman (*Caiman latirostris*), the Spectacled Caiman (*Caiman crocodilus*), a beautiful beast that takes its name from a white bone bridge between its eyes, and the Pantanal's *jacaré* (*Caiman yacare*) which used to be described as a subspecies of the Spectacled Caiman (*Caiman crocodilus yacare*). As for dwarf caimans: they are a different genus altogether.

The *jacaré* of the Pantanal is a medium-sized, short-snouted caiman around 2–2.5m (6.5–8ft) long whose main diet is fish, amphibians, small snakes and birds. It is exceptionally tame – for a crocodile anyway: it is the most common crocodilian species traded as a pet. Tourists in the Pantanal are surprised when they swim in a lagoon and see a caiman observing them from under a water hyacinth, diving away shyly when their eyes meet. But the guides have led them to the right swimming spot: the caimans do not attack large animals like humans and they scare piranhas away.

Courtship occurs during the dry season and, after mating, the female builds her nest from soil and dry vegetation, sharing communally with other females. Each one lays an average of 20–22 eggs during the wet season and they all stay near the nests to protect their eggs from predators. After 90 days the eggs hatch and the juveniles emerge. From then on, one female is in charge of one group of hatchlings – that may not all be hers – which follow her around for protection in and out of the water. Young caimans are yellow with black markings, but as they get older they turn olive-green and lose their black spots. Like chameleons and other reptiles they have the power – though limited – to change their colour at will by the expansion or contraction of special pigment cells, called *melanophores*.

Top Three Dangerous Animals

Ask any visitor what they think the most dangerous animal they are likely to encounter in Brazil is and they are likely to mention piranhas, jaguars, vampire bats and anacondas. Ask the locals and they will give some surprising answers. The most dangerous bird is one of the most beautiful: the **macaw** that will fearlessly protect its nest from any intruder. Diving rapidly downwards, it can split a human skull in two with its mighty beak. The most ferocious aquatic mammal is the **giant otter** that reaches 1.8m (6ft) in length and will boldly come to the aid of any member of its extended family, its growling mouth revealing big sharp teeth (it is not for nothing that it has earned the name 'river wolf').

As for land mammals, beware of the **collared peccary** that will charge and gore a bystander in no time, like a wild boar; the only way of escaping is to climb up the nearest tree.

In the Pantanal you can find all three.

Limerick County Library

The Pantanal and Bonito

Giant otter

The Giant Otter (*Pteronura brasiliensis*) is hard to miss, not just because of its size, but also because it congregates along the banks of slow-flowing, tropical rivers and lagoons in readily observable packs. Each pack is a family group that contains 10–20 individuals and centres around an alpha breeding pair. It has a demarcated territory which it doesn't share with its neighbours. Members of the group groom each other, hunt and play together and, most importantly, support each other when in danger.

These otters' heads are rounded, with small ears, large eyes and a nose that is covered with hair, leaving two oblique slits for nostrils. They have sleek, waterproof brown fur, with a creamy-yellow throat patch, a lithe body, short, stubby legs and webbed feet with sharp claws. They are truly giants: an adult male can reach 1.8m (6ft) including a 0.5m (1.6ft) tail that flattens out like a beaver's. Males weigh about 30kg (66lb); females are about two-thirds that size.

Only jaguars could possibly prey on them, but the group is effective in dissuading any attackers, so for all intents and purposes, they are at the top of the food chain consuming fish, snakes, and even caimans. Their main enemy is man, hunting them for their valuable pelts and driving them almost to extinction in the 1970s and 1980s. Today the species is recovering, but it is still considered endangered.

Mating occurs in the water but the female gives birth in the safety of land. Each group keeps underground family dens where a female produces a litter consisting of one to five cubs after a gestation period of 65–70 days. She leads her young to the water after two

Contact Details for Adventure Operators

Agência Ar: Av. Pilad Rebuá 1184, tel: (67)3255-1008/3255-3330, www.agenciaar.com.br

Bonito Adventure: Av. Pilad Rebua 2066, tel: (67) 3255-3050, www.bonitoadventure.com.br

Carandá Ecotour: Av. Pilad Rebuá 1463, tel: (67) 3255-1695 www.carandatour.com.br

Girasol: Rua Persio Schamann 710, tel: (67) 3255-1297, www.girasolbonito.com.br

Ygarapé Tour: Av. Pilad Rebuá 1853, tel: (67)3255-1733, www.ygarape.com.br

Bonito

months and raises them in the group, looking after them over a period of up to two years. She is very wary of humans and gets so stressed if boats come near her pups that she stops producing milk. For this reason, guides in the Pantanal do not approach any otter nests, especially during the nursing season, and observations are made from afar, using binoculars.

Bonito

On the surface of it, Bonito is a small backwoods town with a population of 18,000 souls at the edge of the Pantanal, where cowboys lead cattle to graze. In reality, it is the hottest eco-destination in South America, with two entries in the Top 10 of Brazilian attractions – including the Number One spot – in a 2007 poll undertaken by the local counterpart of the AA. Even 10 years ago Bonito was hardly known, except amongst the cognoscenti, but word of mouth has spread, and the number of visitors has become so high that the municipality is controlling the numbers to certain popular beauty spots.

There are several attractions around Bonito to keep a visitor hooked for weeks, but the biggest allure is the complete absence of nasties in its transparent streams and lagoons: no piranhas, no leeches, no caimans, no anacondas, no *candiru*, not even the deadly snails carrying schistosomiasis that afflict urban lakes further east. This is a place where one can swim without worry in crystal-clear waters – and with an extraordinary bonus: the fish are remarkably unafraid of humans. As if this were not enough, there are some spectacular caves nearby, one of which, the Gruta do Lago Azul, contains a wondrously blue underground lake.

Best time to go

Visibility in the rivers is best between June and September; the sun enters the Gruta do Lago Azul from the optimum angle between 16 December and 15 January.

How to get there

For years it was difficult to get to Bonito. The nearest airport was 278km (172 miles) away at Campo Grande, which has six daily buses to Bonito, but, like the Pantanal, not all the roads were paved and could be impassable during the height of the

Bonito Statistics

Area: The whole catchment area is a 50 by 50km (31 miles by 31 miles) square above the BR-267, around Bonito which is the centre point of a cross formed by the state highways MS-382 and MS-178.

Rainfall: Same as the Pantanal, but spread more evenly in the year.

Temperature: At an altitude of 315m (1033ft) it gets a bit cooler at night than the Pantanal and the temperature varies between 15°C (59°F) (June–July) and 35°C (95°F) (January–February).

Opposite: The giant otter is top of the aquatic food chain by sheer group protection and care.

The Pantanal and Bonito

Accommodation

Zagaia Eco-resort: The luxury option with quad-bike rentals, spa treatments and fitness rooms. Rodovia Bonito-Três Morros, exit Campo dos Índios, tel: (67) 3255-5601, www.zagaia.com.br

Pousada Águas de Bonito: Spacious, with an agency office offering walking tours, dives, animal viewing and an adventure trail. Rua 29 de Maio 1679, tel: (67) 3255-2330, www.aguasdebonito.com.br

Wetega Hotel: Modern, offers compact tours of the area. Rua Coronel Pilad Rebuá 679, tel: (67) 3325-1333, www.wetegahotel.com.br

Hotel Refúgio: Central, with agency that offers the most comprehensive tours. Rua Nossa Senhora da Penha 366, tel: (67) 3255-1570, www.hotelrefugio.com.br

Hotel Santa Esmeralda: Fantastic setting next to a natural river pool, 17.5km (11 miles) outside Bonito on the old road. Bonito/Guia Lopes, tel: (67) 3255-2683, www.hotel santaesmeralda.com.br

Hotel Pousada Guarany: Has a lot of local colour. Rua Cândido Luis Braga 429, tel: (67) 3255-1990, www.hotelpousadaguarany.com.br

Pousada Arauna: Quiet location off the centre, good value. Rua Monte Castelo 160, tel: (67) 3255-2100, www.hotelarauna.com.br

rainy season (November to April). However, the recent inauguration of a new airport has made travelling to the city much easier.

What to see

Bonito is turning rapidly into the adventure playground of Brazil. Activities are snorkelling and swimming, caving, horse riding, abseiling, whitewater rafting and hiking through the jungle. Also notable is sport fishing, which used to be the main regional pursuit before the tourism explosion.

It is impossible to visit anything without a voucher through a local agency (your hotel can do it for you) and they all have similar prices. If you have children, note that some excursions have a lower age limit, so ask before you book. During the peak season (December/January) you should book any excursions before arriving in Bonito.

Gruta do Lago Azul

This is the must-see of the region, 20km (12 miles) from Bonito, voted Number 8 attraction in Brazil in 2007. After entering a steep cave with overhanging stalactites and descending 90m (295ft) via a series of 300 steps carved into the rock, you reach an underground lake tinted an intense blue by algae. The lighting has to be right for the full effect and this only occurs in the early morning between 08:00 and 09:00. There is a small and fragile ecosystem inside the lake so numbers are strictly controlled and even dipping a finger into the water is prohibited. Children under five years old are not allowed inside. (Entry 07:00–14:00, R$10).

Gruta de São Miguel

This is a much deeper (180m/590ft) and equally interesting cave 16km (10 miles) from Bonito that is reached via a suspension treetop walkway suitable for bird-watching. During the two-hour walk inside you can observe Barn Owls (*Tyto alba*) and various types of bats. There are elevator cars that take you back up to the entrance and a short jungle trail. Open 07:00–17:00 in the summer (limit 285 visitors per day) and 08:00–16:00 in the winter (limit reduced to 255 persons). Entry fee R$18.

Bonito

Buraca das Araras

This is a large caldera 100m (328ft) deep and 500m (1640ft) in diameter discovered only in 1912 near Jardim, a small town 58km (36 miles) away. One can abseil or walk down a steep trail to the bottom that is brimming with dense jungle vegetation. It is the home of a great number of scarlet macaws (*araras*) which return en masse before sunset. Entry by tour only.

Rio da Prata

This is Bonito's *tour de force*, voted the top attraction in Brazil in 2007. After a 54km (33-mile) drive followed by a short 40-minute walk by the course of the Rio de Prata through *mata ciliar*, you reach its headwaters where you can snorkel amongst the region's fish: *dourados*, *piraputangas*, *piaus*, *corimbas* and *pacus*. They show up, alright: the locals make sure by crumbling bread or by throwing corn in the water. If swimming with dolphins is a unique experience, then swimming with large catfish that come straight up to your goggles and breathe through their gills, relaxed and curious, is positively surreal. Remarkably for a river, it is also possible to go scuba diving – to a depth of 3–6m (10–20ft). Entrance by tour only.

Abismo das Anhumas

This is the big adventure and you have to overcome several obstacles even to join in: you have to be over 18; you have to take a course; if you fail, you are not accepted. Despite all this, and the $300 price tag, there is always a waiting list. You first abseil for 72m (236ft) down into a cave, then you hike through the stalactites and stalagmites to an underground lake where you go snorkelling. Simply extraordinary.

The birds of the Pantanal

Like all wetlands, the Pantanal is teeming with bird life. Many birds are aquatic, such as the light brown Brazilian Teal (*Amazonetta brasiliensis*) that lives paired in large groups and builds nests made of leaves that float freely on the water. Another is the Anhinga, or 'snakebird' (*Anhinga anhinga*), a darter species with a grey-black body 85cm (33in) long and a wingspan of 1.15m (4ft). It gets its common name from its elongated s-shaped neck that is often seen above water like a snake ready to strike. It possesses a sharp

More Activities

Balneário Municipal
This is the only place where you can just turn up without a voucher. Crystal clear and full of tropical multicoloured fish, it feels like having an illicit dip inside an aquarium. Open 07:00–18:00, entry R$10.

Cachoeiras do Rio Peixe
This is a four-hour jungle trail in a private *fazenda*, 36km (22 miles) from Bonito, going from waterfall to waterfall where you can swim and have the cascading water pummel and massage your body. Entrance to the *fazenda* is by appointment or by tour that includes entry fee and lunch.

Parque das Cachoeiras
Only 16km (10 miles) away from Bonito, there is a 'waterfall park' on the Rio Mimoso, with six springs next to each other, a more sedate, family-friendly version of the Rio Peixe experience. It is private, and it is open 08:00–16:00. The entry fee varies between R$20 and R$32 depending on the season.

Boca da Onça
This is the largest waterfall in the Mato Grosso do Sul, the 156m (512ft) 'Jaguar's Mouth' at the source of the Rio Salobra. It is reached via a 3km (2-mile) medium-difficult trail.

The Pantanal and Bonito

Kadiwéu Villages and Art Gallery

The Kadiwéu are the last tribe that belonged to the Guaikurú, a bloodthirsty warrior folk that enslaved all neighbouring tribes before the arrival of the Europeans. They were tall and handsome but had a fearsome reputation, practising infanticide and performing blood-letting during body-piercing ceremonies. They resisted the Portuguese valiantly until the 19th century, having learned to breed and ride the introduced horses. They galloped into battle hanging by the side of their charges, a feat that inspired a famous aquarelle painting by Debret (1822). They are now peaceful, number about 1500 souls and live in the Campina and Bodoquena villages, about 80km (50 miles) away from Bonito; the latter is more easily reached from the MS-339. They make abstract, brightly coloured decorative pottery which they exhibit and sell in Bonito's Casa do Artesão in Rua Coronel Pilad Rebuá next to the City Council. (Open 08:00–11:00 and 14:00–18:00, free entry).

bill that spears fish which it then flips in the air and swallows whole. It doesn't have any waterproof glands so its plumage gets wet, which is why it is often seen perched in a tree with its wings open to dry. The flipside of this is that it can dive more easily; it can spend several minutes underwater.

Another abundant species that is not often seen inland is the Neotropical Cormorant (*Phalacrocorax olivaceus*) which, at 64cm (26 in) long and a 100cm (39 in) wingspan, is smaller than the anhinga but subsists on the same diet. It is a monogamous bird that nests together with its mate and sometimes hunts in gaggles, trying to drive fish to the shallows.

Even smaller at 55–60cm (21–23 in), but with a larger wingspan of 1.25m (4ft), is the Southern or Crested Caracara (*Caracara plancus*), one of the main raptors of the Pantanal. It is also a scavenger, often seen walking on the ground looking for carrion to eat. A farmer's friend, it often picks ticks from cattle and has adapted to living close to man. Its black crest resting on its white head like a Mohican and its orange-grey crooked beak make it very conspicuous. These also help distinguish it from its cousin, the Yellow-headed Caracara (*Milvago chimachima*), that looks much more like a falcon.

Other common birds of prey include the gregarious Snail Kite (*Rostrhamus sociabilis*), a 45cm (18 in) brown bird that flies head downwards looking for snails, and, perched on small earth mounds, the Burrowing Owl (*Athene cunicularia*) a 20cm (8 in) underground-nesting yellow-brown owl with no ear tufts that is active during the day and surprisingly approachable.

The Guira (*Guira guira*) is a Brazilian type of cuckoo, 40cm (16 in) long, with a greyish-brown streaked plumage and a protruding hairy tuft; it is common everywhere in Brazil, but it seems to shun the Amazon. Unlike the cuckoo, it doesn't leave its eggs in other birds' nests, but it has an equally strange reproductive behaviour: males and females mate together in groups and lay eggs in joint nests where both paternity and maternity are indeterminate. As a result, or maybe because of it, incidents of egg desertion and even infanticide are not uncommon. The other bird that nests communally like the guira is its cousin, the Smooth-billed Ani

The birds of the Pantanal

(*Crotophaga ani*), which is of similar size but bluish-black and is often seen preening itself high in the trees.

Maybe the strangest-looking bird is the Roseate Spoonbill (*Ajaja ajaja*), which is a wading bird with vivid bright-pink feathers and a flattened grey bill that spreads out like a spatula or a spoon. It uses its tip to poke about in the swampy water and detect food such as fish and crustaceans. These birds are square and long-legged, measuring 80cm tall by 80 cm long (31 in by 31 in), a bill length of 15–18cm (6–7in) and a wingspan of 120cm (47in), which makes their dismissive nickname of 'pink chickens' rather ill-founded. As they stand in the water balancing on one leg, they look more like squat flamingoes.

The Wattled Jacana (*Jacana jacana*) is another unmistakeable denizen of the swamplands. No one can miss its cinnamon-brown back and wings, black neck and chest, yellow bill topped by a red wattle, grey, long stilt-like legs and long toes. These help it balance itself on the large leaves of the floating vegetation it wades on, as it forages for insects and seeds. In this species it is the female that mates with many males and it is the male that incubates the eggs and takes care of the chicks, sometimes carrying them on its wings while running away from danger.

Above: *The jabiru stork is the photogenic conservation symbol of the Pantanal.*

But it is the conspicuous Jabiru Stork (*Jabiru mycteria*) that has become the symbol of the region. It is a big, beautiful bird, 1.2m (4ft) high with a 30cm (12in) slender bill and a wingspan of 2.5m (8ft). Its colour is white with a black, almost bare head and a distinctive burgundy spot on its throat. As big as a rhea, it is the largest flying bird in Brazil and can soar gracefully to very high altitudes. It eats fish, molluscs and amphibians but does not shy away from carrion, eating the dead fish that have been stranded when the waters start ebbing from the shallows. The female only makes the one nest to which she returns every year to lay her eggs.

Common Neotropical monkeys

The monkeys of the New World differ from their Old World cousins in two fundamental aspects: they have long, prehensile tails that allow them to hang from trees, and their noses are flat with nostrils that face outwards sideways, rather than downwards; man,

The Pantanal and Bonito

Howler Antics

Like many wild Neotropical monkeys, howlers dislike humans and will throw fruit and stones at them from up high; if that doesn't scare their pursuers they will urinate on them and finally throw their excrement with uncanny accuracy. If you do want to photograph the howlers, you are advised to use a long zoom lens.

Below: Capuchin monkeys, maybe the most intelligent monkeys in the world, are being employed by some police forces in the USA.

having evolved from the Old World primates, matches them in these characteristics.

The capuchin monkeys (*Cebus sp.*) are by far the most common species seen in Brazil; the tuft of black hair on their heads reminded the first explorers of the Capuchin monks' caps. The Brown Capuchin (*Cebus apella*), whose fur is brown/black but can fade to yellow on the underbelly, is the most widespread species and can be seen in almost any biome that has a forest. Brown capuchins tend to curl their long tails in a coil and use them to move about noisily from branch to branch. They forage mostly for fruit, but they also eat insects, reptiles, birds and mice. A troop is composed of almost twice as many females as males and the adults are generally promiscuous within the troop. Females gives birth to a single baby after a gestation period of 160 days and everyone is very tolerant and protective of the juveniles.

Capuchin monkeys are among the most intelligent animals around, and their ranks used to provide the traditional 'organ grinder' monkeys of times past. They have been trained to be companions to paraplegics, and they can be instructed to serve food, switch lights on and off and count to nine. US police are investigating whether they can use them for dangerous reconnaissance and intelligence work.

No book on Brazil could be complete without a mention of the howler monkeys (*Alouatta sp.*), which are also widespread and comprise eight species, all bearded and with thick, hairy fur. The ones you are more likely to encounter are the Red-handed Howlers (*Alouatta belzebul*), which are black, apart from their limbs and tails that are deeply red; the Black Howlers (*Alouatta caraya*), which are more common in the south of Brazil; and the Brown Howler Monkeys (*Alouatta fusca*) in the southeastern Mata Atlântica.

Common Neotropical monkeys

Their adult length ranges from 55cm (21 in) to about 90cm (35 in), plus a prehensile tail equal in length to their body, and they weigh between 7 and 10kg (15–22 lb). They all live in the forest canopy and, although omnivorous, they eat mostly leaves and fruit. Their sexual behaviour is similar to that of the capuchins.

As their name implies, howlers are famous for their loud growls that are heard at sunrise and sunset and are often mistaken for the furious roars of an angry jaguar. In reality, they are calls from the males of the troop to establish the limits of its territory. (In zoos, taped calls from another troop that sounds far away are employed to trick the howlers into settling down). The males can enlarge their voice boxes up to three times their normal size and special shell-like resonating organs in their tracheas enable them to be heard up to 5km (3 miles) away, a fact that labels them as the loudest animals in existence. This quality has cost them dearly: locals hunt them for bush meat but especially for their throat sacs, which are so elastic and flexible that they are used to carry water or are crafted into handbags.

Birds Translated

English name	Brazilian name	Scientific name
Anhinga or Snakebird	Anhinga	*Anhinga anhing*
Brazilian Teals	Ananaí	*Amazonetta brasiliensis*
Burrowing Owl	Coruja-buraqueira	*Athene cunicularia*
Guira	Anu-branco	*Guira guira*
Hyacinthe Macaw	Arara-azul	*Anodorhynchus hyacinthinus*
Jabiru Stork	Jabiru	*Jabiru mycteria*
Neotropical Cormorant	Biguá	*Phalacrocorax olivaceus*
Roseate Spoonbill	Colhereiro	*Ajaja ajaja*
Smooth-billed Ani	Anu-preto	*Crotophaga ani*
Snail Kite	Caramujeiro	*Rostrhamus sociabilis*
Southern or Crested Caracara	Caracará	*Caracara plancus*
Wattled Jacana	Jacanã	*Jacana jacana*
Yellow-headed Caracara	Gavião-carrapateiro	*Milvago chimachima*

MATA ATLÂNTICA: IGUAÇU

Iguaçu National Park, shared with Argentina, is one of Brazil's top tourist destinations, second only to Rio de Janeiro. As the name implies – it means 'Great Waters' in the local Tupi-Guarani language – the park is centred upon of the world's most imposing waterfalls. At 72m (236ft) high they are not the world's tallest – the title belongs to Angel Falls in Venezuela; at 2700m (8859ft) wide they are not the world's widest – this title belongs to the Chute de Khone in Laos; and at 1000 m³/s they rank only eleventh with respect to maximum rate of flow. Yet, everyone who has admired the crescent of the 270 distinct cascades surrounded by the plushest of vegetation supports their claim to be the most photogenic. This is mainly due to the flat, vast mesa, flooded by the Iguaçu River before it reaches the edge of the cliffs. The horizon extends as far as the eye can see, blending the blue from the sky, the deep green of the foliage and the brilliant white of the falls into a seemingly endless, breathtaking arrangement.

The falls themselves are situated at the confluence of the Rio Paraná with the Rio Iguaçu which, over 1300km (808 miles), drains the most southern part of Brazil's coastal mountain range, the Serra do Mar. They lie in the westernmost point of the state of Paraná near the triple border point with Argentina and Paraguay. The best panoramic views of the falls are from the Brazilian side, but more intimate close-up views of the individual waterfalls are to be had on the Argentinian side.

Bird Life

Saffron Toucanet
Black-fronted Piping-guan
Helmeted Woodpecker
Russet-winged Spadebill
Red-breasted and Toco Toucans

Opposite, top to bottom:
The Iguaçu Falls; a male
White-bearded Manakin;
a capybara family.

Mata Atlântica: Iguaçu

Park Statistics

Area: 2250km² (868 sq miles), out of which 1853km² (715 sq miles) are in Brazil.
Rainfall: It varies between 1500mm (59 in) and 1750mm (69 in), but the climate is extremely humid all year around.
Temperature: It varies widely from 0–40°C (32–104°F), averaging 18–22°C (34–72°F) for most of the year. The humidity can make the heat very uncomfortable.
Opening Times: From April to September, from 09:00–17:00; October to March from 09:00–18:00. Adult tickets cost R$12 while children under seven years old enter free. Brazilian nationals, locals and Mercosul citizens (belonging to Argentina, Paraguay and Uruguay) enjoy a variety of discounts. There are two park entrances, one on the Brazilian side and one on the Argentinian side. Buses leave regularly from Foz to the Argentinian Park entrance (08:00–19:00 daily, entry US$10). Border controls are minimal, and passports are inspected on board the buses. In order to minimize ecological damage, reduce emissions, noise and pollution and maximize the number of visitors per vehicle, the transport system inside the Brazilian section is by public double-decker buses only (R$5; children pay regardless of age).

Parque Nacional do Iguaçu

The park was listed as a UNESCO World Heritage Site in 1985 and provides an island of original Mata Atlântica in the South American continent's second largest hydrographic basin, the Paraná-Plata, which is increasingly being lost to logging and agriculture. This is composed of araucaria trees that predominate above an altitude of 600m (1969ft), seasonal semi-deciduous forest between 300 and 500m (984–1641ft) and palm vegetation in the lower elevations, along with epiphytes such as liana vines, orchids and bromeliads. By the rivers you can walk under the sail-like canopies of Queen palms (*Cocos plumosa*); Guabirovas (*Campomanesia xanthocarpa*) trees of the myrtle family; Ingás – large, attractive trees one of which, *Inga edulis*, produces a pod with seeds protected by a thick white foam that tastes remarkably like vanilla ice-cream; various tree ferns and Paraná *Peltophorum* species such as the graceful Yellow Poinciana (*Peltophorum dubium*) with its fine bipinnate leaves.

The park includes 2000 species of plants, 68 species of mammals, 38 of reptiles, and 18 of amphibians, and the trees are teeming with 422 species of birds. Another special feature of the park are the 300 species of butterflies that flutter constantly in its paths, including the Blue Morpho (*Morpho menelaus*), whose cobalt blue metallic sheen once seen is never forgotten.

There are several species of reptiles such as adders and coral snakes, but in order to spot any of them you have to go far away from the crowds.

The visitors' area is managed by a private-public corporation established in 1999 and the popularity of the falls along with the advent of private investment have ensured that the park enjoys the widest range of infrastructure than any other in Brazil or, indeed, in South America. There are paved roads, modern facilities and special tourist attractions such as boat and train rides, as well as an Environmental Education school that provides lectures and organizes events. Inside the park, there are souvenir shops, observation platforms, fast-food bars, cafeterias (open during opening times) and a swish 400-seater restaurant at Porto Canoas serving meals from 12:00–16:00. All in all, you are more

Parque Nacional do Iguaçu

likely to have a North American-style experience here than in any other national park in Brazil.

As the park is shared between Argentina and Brazil, you may see or hear two ways of spelling and pronouncing its name. In Portuguese it is spelled Iguaçu (pronounced Ee-gua-SSU) and in Spanish Iguazú. This bilingualism extends to the names of the attractions (e.g. Garganta do Diablo/del Diablo, Porto/Puerto

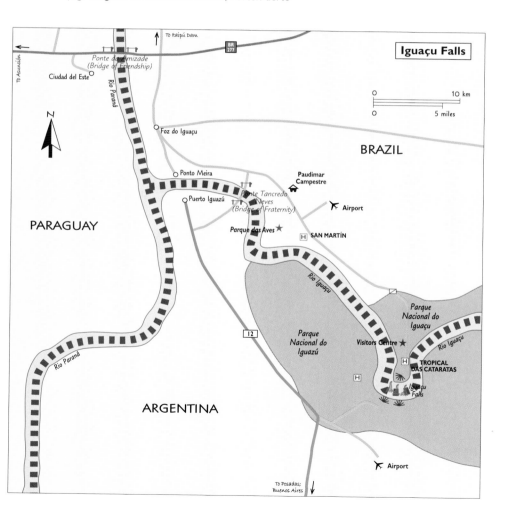

Mata Atlântica: Iguaçu

Accommodation

The Rodovia das Cataratas from Foz to the national park is full of hotels.

Bourbon Resort and Convention Centre: This is the top business hotel. Rodovia das Cataratas Km 2.5, tel: (45) 3529-0123, reservations: 0800-45-1010, www.bourbon.com.br

Tropical das Cataratas: One of the most famous hotels in the world, it has the best views of the falls. This is a 1950s colonial-style building that deserves its hype. Rodovia das Cataratas 24.5km. Booking online or tel: 0810-444-2822 or (45) 3757-421OO, www.hotelcataratas.com

San Martín: Rodovia das Cataratas Km 17. Reservations: 0800-45-4555, http://hotelsanmartin.com.br

Bristol Carimã (in the park): Rodovia das Cataratas Km 10.5, tel: (45) 3521-3000, www.carima.com.br

Hostel Paudimar Campestre: Only 2km (1 mile) from the national park entrance, this is an excellent hostel with a swimming pool and a large garden and playing field. They organize cheap day tours to the Argentinian side. Rodovia das Cataratas Km 12.5, Remanso Grande, tel: (45) 3529-6061, www.paudimar.com.br

Canoas). In this book, the Portuguese names and spellings are used throughout.

Best time to go

This is a year-round destination, but the falls are at their most majestic at the end of the rainy season during December–February. The wettest months are September–October and the driest July–August when there are only 150 individual cataracts. The best times for taking photographs are early morning and sunset on the Brazilian side and afternoon on the Argentinian side.

How to get there

The nearest city on the Brazilian side is Foz do Iguaçu – generally abbreviated to Foz – which is connected to the park by the BR-469 highway, named the Rodovia das Cataratas. The entrance gate is on Km 18 and visitors need to travel 12km (7 miles) inside the park to reach the falls. Most visitors arrive by air to the Foz do Iguaçu international airport, which is served by regular flights.

Curitiba, the state capital, is 668km (415 miles) away from Foz on the paved and well-maintained BR-277 highway.

The nearest city on the Argentinian side is Puerto Iguazú (population: 30,000), which is much smaller than Foz (population: 300,000), but is closer to the park itself.

Situated at the end of the BR-275, the Bridge of Friendship across the Rio Paraná joins Brazil with Ciudad del Este in Paraguay and the highway continues on to Asunción as Ruta 2. The Bridge of Fraternity/Tancredo Neves across the Iguaçu River joins Brazil with Argentina and on to Ruta 12 to Buenos Aires.

Where to go

The ways you can see the falls depend on your inclination and your budget, and all hotels can organize trips for you.

On foot

There are several trails that take you close to the falls and offer access to the animals and particularly the birds and butterflies of the park. Note that, however much you try to stay dry, the spray will get you wet, so dress in light clothes and wrap your watches, films, cameras and any electrical gadgets such as iPods in plastic. You might like to consider buying a waterproof disposable camera and, should you wish to take the boat rides, bringing along a change of clothes.

There are three main trails on the Brazilian side. The **Hotel Tropical das Cataratas** trail starts opposite Hotel Cataratas and is a short, steep 1.2km (0.7-mile) descent to a platform at the bottom of the Iguaçu River opposite the Garganta do Diablo main waterfall (Devil's Throat) where there is a small café. If you are not sufficiently mobile you can take the two 27m (88ft) high panoramic elevators to the Naipi platform where there are also ramps for wheelchairs.

It is important to remember that the falls are but a small part of the national park and that there are several long jungle trails that are worthwhile in themselves. The park bus can leave you at the beginning of both of the trails below.

The **Poço Preto (Black Well)** trail is the most eco-friendly of the trails, where you hike a good 9km (5.5 miles) – one way – on foot, bicycle or electric buggy. In this way you can observe intimately the fauna and flora of the park, in particular its orchids and bromeliads and understorey birds that fly not too far off from the ground, such as the White-bearded Manakin (*Manacus manacus*), the Magpie Tanager (*Neothraupis fasciata*), the Plush-crested Jay (*Cyanocorax chrysops*), the Yellow Tyrannulet (*Capsiempis flaveola*), the Green-headed Tanager (*Tangara seledon*), the Black-throated Trogon (*Trogon rufus*) and many others.

This trail starts at the left of the park entrance on the BR-469, and it does not involve seeing much of the falls. At the bottom there is a short 500m (547yd) walk to a 10m (33ft) high observation tower over the Lagoa do Jacaré do Poço Preto where you may observe some of the park's aquatic and semi-aquatic fauna like caimans or capybaras. You can then opt to go by boat or kayak to the Ilhas da Taquara (Bamboo Islands). It is safe to go swimming and snorkelling, but do note that the water is cold year-round. Try to fit in the Ilha dos Papagaios (Parrot Island), where hundreds of parrots leave at sunrise and return at sunset. The guided trail lasts four to five hours with departures from 08:00 until 15:00.

Accommodation in Foz

In Foz most hotels are much cheaper and there are regular buses to the entrance of the park.
San Juan: Rua Marechal Deodoro 1349, tel: (45) 3523-1512, www.sanjuanhoteis.com.br
Foz de Iguaçu: Av Brasil 97, tel: (45) 3523-4455, http://fozdoiguacu.com.br
Foz Plaza: Rua Marechal Deodoro 1819. Reservations: 0800-11-6768, www.fozplaza.com.br

The **Bananeiras (Banana tree)** trail is a short 2km (1-mile) walk starting further down the BR-469 and passing by small waterholes to observe the birds such as the Slaty-breasted Wood-rail (*Aramides saracura*), the Wattled Jacana (*Jacana Jacana*), the Snail Kite (*Rostrhamus sociabilis*), Green Ibis (*Mesembrinibis cayennensis*), the River Warbler (*Phaeothlypis rivularis*), the Ringed Kingfisher (*Ceryle torquatus*) and the Greater Ani (*Crotophaga major*). At the end of the trail you can take a boat to Ilhas da Taquara and/or return to Porto Canoas. The guided walk lasts for approximately 2.5 hours and starts every half an hour.

A popular option is the **Macuco Safari** operated by Macuco Ecoaventura (www.macucoecoaventura.com.br) that is signposted halfway between the two trails above the BR-469. It combines a 3km (2-mile) drive in an open-carriage vehicle, a walk, a shower at the tame Macuco Waterfall and a 4km (3-mile) short but thrilling rafting ride down the Iguaçu River rapids.

Below: On the Argentinian side narrow plank gangways with steep steps come very close to the Iguaçu Falls; take care if you suffer from vertigo.

You need around four hours to walk all the short trails by the falls on the Argentinian side: the Circuito Superior (Upper circuit), Circuito Inferior (Lower circuit), Devil's Throat trail and the San Martín Island. They all bring you up close to the falls so expect to be wet, but, because of their popularity, there is hardly any wildlife to be seen.

The **Lower Circuit** is 1.7km (1 mile) and the footpath (raised 50cm/ 19 in from the ground) starts from the old observation tower and has eight platforms with the ultimate close-up views. This is the most humid part of the park, because the closed canopy acts like a giant greenhouse. In

Parque Nacional do Iguaçu

compensation, this is the trail to take in order to admire the butterflies, because they are attracted by human sweat. The birds that you encounter here are small larvae- and insect-eaters such as the Tufted Antshrike (*Mackenziaena severa*), the Large-tailed Antshrike (*Mackenziaena leachii*), the Rufous Gnateater (*Conopophaga lineata*) and the ubiquitous Fuscous Flycatcher (*Cnemotriccus fuscatus*).

The **Upper Circuit** covers the top areas of the Dos Hermanas, Chico, Ramírez , Bosseti, Adam and Eve, Bernabé Mendez and Mbiguá waterfalls with six wide balcony points. There is also a viewing area opposite the crescent formed by the San Martín, Escondido, Dos Mosqueteros, Rivadavia and Tres Mosqueteros waterfalls. By the Ramírez cascade you can take a free five-minute ride to the Island of San Martín to pick up the **San Martín Island Trail**. This is 650m (711yd) long and begins by climbing 172 stone steps to reach some excellent views of the San Martín and Devil's Throat falls, as well as the natural La Ventana rock formation. This is a very photogenic spot, second only to the Hotel Tropical das Cataratas trail, and featured in Roland Joffé's Oscar-winning film *The Mission*.

The **Devil's Throat trail** (1.1km/0.6 miles) is a must, as it ends by the catwalk that allows access to the Garganta do Diablo and a vertical view over the edge of the mightiest of the Iguaçu cataracts. This is the moment that will be indelibly stamped in your mind, as all your senses are overpowered by the roar of the falls, the musky smell and moist aftertaste of the prevailing dampness, and the frightful sight of the sheer abyss below.

Train trips

A British-built, narrow-gauge slow train powered by compressed gas which has a low environmental impact, runs between the Argentinian Visitors' Centre and the Garganta do Diablo waterfall. It leaves every 30 minutes and can transport 150 passengers with a maximum speed of 20km/hr (12 miles/hr). It stops at Cataratas station (1.5km/0.9 miles) which connects with the Upper and Lower Circuit trails, the Sheraton and a café. The final stop is at the Garganta do Diablo (4km/3 miles), a short walk to the viewing platform.

Mata Atlântica: Iguaçu

Boat trips

At the bottom of the Lower Circuit on the Argentinian side, at Porto Canoas, there is a landing dock. Large speedboats take you through the gorge that separates the Ilha San Martín from the waterfall cliff edge. The operators provide you with waterproof gear and bags for your cameras and valuables (including your passports).

You can also take a motor boat downriver to the Ilhas da Taquara and to the ends of the Bananeiras and Poço Preto trails to walk them in reverse and end up on the Brazilian side.

Rafting

It may seem unbelievable, looking at the power of the waterfall, but you can go rafting down the Iguaçu River, because the falls lie on a bend that quickly tames their force. This involves a 30-minute 2km (1-mile) ride on the rapids and 2km (1 mile) on calm waters. The rapids are rated medium level (class III+) and are recommended for visitors over 14 years of age. You can arrange this at Km 25 of the Rodovia das Cataratas daily from 08:00–17:00 (to 18:00 during the summer).

Helicopter trips

The **Helisul Táxi Aéreo** company operates some outstanding heli-tours. They are not exactly eco-friendly but they may be the only way to appreciate the width and drama of the Iguaçu Falls. There is a minimum of three passengers and the trips range from seven minutes (falls only), 10 minutes (falls and national park) or 30 minutes (falls, park and Itaipú Dam). Contact them at Rodovia das Cataratas, Km 16.5, tel: (45) 3529-7474, www.helisul.com

Other sights nearby
Parque das Aves

On Km 17.1 of the Rodovia das Cataratas lies this 17ha (42-acre) private park with 500 species of birds in large enclosures, including a walk-in aviary for butterflies and hummingbirds, a Pantanal aviary, plus reptile sections with anacondas and caimans. It features a restaurant and a souvenir shop. Entry is US$10 (US dollars) and it is open daily from 08:30–17:30 (winter) and from 08:30–18:00 (summer). Allow at least 1.5 hours for your visit. For more information visit www.parquedasaves.com.br

Other sights nearby

Itaipú Dam

The statue of Christ the Redeemer in Rio may have been deemed one of the Seven Wonders of the Modern World by popular vote, but it is the Itaipú Dam that was chosen in 1994 by the American Society of Civil Engineers as one of its Seven Engineering Wonders of the Modern World – along with the Channel Tunnel, the Golden Gate Bridge and the Panama Canal. For those who want to temper ecology with technology, a trip to the Visitors' Centre at Avenida Tancredo Neves 6702, 15km (9 miles) upwards from the Friendship Bridge, is an agreeable choice.

Itaipú can certainly lay claim to being one of the biggest engineering feats in history. A multinational consortium started construction in 1970 and, in the course of its construction, diverted the course of the Paraná River – the seventh largest in the world – by digging a 2km (1.2-mile) bypass and shifting a volume of earth and rocks more than eight times greater than that for the Channel Tunnel. The flooded basin resulted in a reservoir with an area of 1350km^2 (521 sq miles) that is now used for water sports. The dam itself is 7744m (8469yd) long and 196m (643ft) high at its highest point with enough concrete to build 210 football stadiums as big as Rio's Maracanã. Its capacity in 2006 satisfied 20% of the Brazilian consumption of electricity and 95% of the Paraguayan demand.

Opening times are daily from 08:00–17:00 (18:00 in the summer). There are various types of tours with increasing levels of access on different days and times. The most popular one is, unsurprisingly, the 'tourist' tour which is free but short. If you are more interested and have extra time to spend, you can take the 'panoramic' tour that costs R$17 or the 'special' tour that costs R$30. (There is a 50% discount for children under 16 and seniors over 60. Children under seven years are admitted free.) On Friday and Saturday evenings, there is a Sound and Vision show at 20:30, R$6. For more information visit www.itaipu.gov.br

The Capybara

The Capybara (*Hydrochaeris hydrochaeris*) is the world's largest rodent, a stocky animal that measures 1–1.3m (3–4ft) in length, is 50–60cm (20–42in) tall and can weigh up to 80kg (176lb). If you think that is a big rodent, note that fossils have been found of a

In Danger

Inconceivable as it may seem, the world-famous Iguaçu National Park was temporarily put in the Heritage Danger List by UNESCO in 1997. In May that year, a group of 800-odd local residents occupied the section of an old colonial road, blocked since 1986, that runs for 18km (11 miles) inside the park. They illegally started work to reopen the overgrown path, so that local villagers could hunt and fish inside the protected areas. The local support for the squatters was such that the park authorities were unable to react. The impasse continued for four whole years, causing a rift with UNESCO, until the Brazilian Federal government forcibly closed the road in June 2001 and replanted cleared forest.

Mata Atlântica: Iguaçu

How to Spell Iguaçu

The spelling of the town and the national park with a cedilla, 'ç', divided the town of Foz in October 2005. That was when the local council approved proposal 65/2005 to change the spelling to the more English-friendly Iguassu. Deputy Djalma Pastorelo, who introduced the motion, pointed out that half of the visitors to the park are from abroad, that Internet search engines do not accept cedillas, that even the website of the prefecture is the ugly-looking www.fozdoiguacu.pr.gov.br (with a 'c') and that the original spelling of the town was with double 's' anyway, before the Portuguese orthographic reform of 1945. Nevertheless, the furore this proposition caused in the town of Foz – and in Brazil as a whole – caused mayor Paulo MacDonald Ghisi to ask for a consultation exercise. With polls recording a 91% disapproval rating for the measure and after a bad-tempered public meeting where opponents outnumbered supporters by 4:1, he eventually vetoed the proposal in November 2005.

giant prehistoric capybara that was larger than a bear. It is hypothesized that such gigantism is not the result of a lack of predators – it is being preyed upon by almost every carnivore in the jungle – but the lack of competitor species.

Capybaras have a square head, piggy eyes and small ears that are high on the head so that they can stick out of the water. The face ends in a blunt muzzle, not unlike a bull terrier's. They have no tails and are covered in thick rusty brown hair that turns quite dark when wet. Like ducks, their legs are short and their toes are webbed, indicative of their semi-aquatic nature: they are excellent swimmers, running readily to the water to escape from danger. They even sleep in the water for safety, floating low with only their nostrils emerging, like hippos; indeed, they occupy the same biological niche in the tropics of South America as hippos do in Africa.

They aggregate in herds that average 10–20 animals (but can on occasion be as many as 40) in order to graze in the banks of the creeks, lakes and swamps of tropical South America – their very name means 'Master of the Grass' in Tupi-Guarani. In line with other rodents, their front teeth never cease growing to make up for the wear and tear of their diet. They feed in the morning and early evening, preferring to spend most of the hot day cooling off in the water and communicating with each other using a wide spectrum of purrs, barks and yelps. The group revolves around a dominant alpha male who marks his territory with a sebaceous gland on his nose. Mating takes place – where else? – in the water and, after a gestation of 150–160 days, the female gives birth to a litter of four to seven babies. Interestingly, the young are able to eat grasses within a week, even while they are still suckling. They receive their milk not only from their mother but also from other helper females in the group.

Although in the past they have been hunted for their meat and their fur, strict protection laws as well as their breeding behaviour have ensured that their current survival is of no concern.

The Coati

It is well nigh impossible for a visitor to the Iguaçu National Park not to come face-to-face with a South American Coati (*Nasua nasua*); they have grown fairly tame and fearless and approach the

The Coati

tourists for food (do not feed them – many park animals suffer from obesity, high cholesterol and diabetes). At first glance, they resemble their close relatives, the North American raccoons. They are about 1–1.4m (3–4.5ft) long and about 30cm (12 in) tall with spotted eyes, a brownish-grey back, white belly and a long, bushy ringed tail that makes up a good third of their length. But it is their long, flexible, slightly upward noses that give the game away. When coatis follow almost next to the heels of tourists they will nuzzle their way on the ground like wild pigs; they tuck their noses under their bellies when they go to sleep.

Above: *Male coatis can be easily identified because they are solitary foragers.*

Coatis have strong bear-like paws and are excellent tree climbers, using their long tails for balance. Like margays, they can bend their ankles to descend from trees head-first. They forage on the ground during the day but retire to tree branches to sleep, mate, and, in the case of females, to nest and give birth. They tend to live close to humans, sometimes rummaging on rubbish. This connection with humans appears to work on a more fundamental level and may be a defence against their many predators. They are omnivorous, eating anything from leaves and fruit to birds' eggs, insects, lizards and rodents. They have been known to raid chicken coops rural areas, like foxes, and even eat carrion, should they chance upon it.

The sexes lead segregated lives. Females and their young live loosely in groups of 5–25 individuals, while males live a solitary life. In the past, males, who are also twice the size of females, were thought to be a different species called *Coati mundi*. During the

Mata Atlântica: Iguaçu

breeding season, which normally corresponds to the start of the rainy season, a male will be allowed to join a female party and become the only one to mate with its members. Afterwards he will depart, while each female leaves to build her nest high up on the canopy, give birth and nurse her young. Gestation is around 75 days and a litter consists of about three to seven young which are altricial, that is they are naked, blind and totally dependent on their mother for survival. Once they are able to walk and climb trees, the mother and her babies rejoin the female-only group.

Coatis are curious and intelligent animals and display good cognitive skills in captivity. They recognize each other not only through smell but also by appearance and voice, and use a repertoire of sounds and postures to communicate with each other.

Because they help control populations of insects and rodents, their impact on humans is positive and they are occasionally kept as pets. Farmers, however, consider them as pests and shoot them illegally, because they raid their crops and take their chickens. This and habitat destruction have added to the reduction in their numbers but, thanks to their considerable adaptability, they are not threatened as yet.

The origin of the falls

You may prefer to think that the formation of the falls started almost 200 million years ago when Africa and South America started drifting apart, a geological milestone that caused fissures in the middle of the South American continent. Among the Iguaçu River waters, you can still see the volcanic overflows and the basaltic bedrock that was subsequently subject to aquatic erosion. Alternatively, you may wish to opt for the local Guarani myth.

Once upon a time there was a Kaingang Indian village by the banks of the Iguaçu River whose chief, Igobi, was wise and kind. He had a daughter, called Naipi, whose beauty was so astounding that when she went bathing, the river stood still to admire her figure. The chief looked at his daughter with affection and pride but was saddened because he knew that no human could possess her. According to custom, she was worthy only as the wife of a god.

The origin of the falls

The time came for Naipi to be sacrificed to the serpent god Mboi, mighty god of Earthquakes, son of Tupã, the Lord of Heaven and Earth. But the night before, she eloped with Tarobá, the bravest warrior of the tribe, with whom she had fallen in love. The two lovers stole a dugout pirogue and started paddling away from the village. When the serpent god found out that Naipi had disappeared with a human, he became wild with jealousy and burrowed out of the innards of the earth, forming the cleft of the falls and overturning the pirogue of the lovers who were enveloped by the river.

Naipi was turned into a large rock in the Devil's Throat, doomed to be whipped by the waters for all eternity. Tarobá became the palm that leans by the edge of the abyss, forever lamenting his lost love; and as for Mboi – he is hidden in a cave behind the sheet of water, making sure that no one will dare bring the lovers back to life again.

Birds Translated

English name	Brazilian name	Scientific name
Black-fronted Piping-Guan	Jacutinga	Pipile jacutinga
Black-throated Trogon	Surucuá-de-barriga-amarela	Trogon rufus
Fuscous Flycatcher	Guaracavuçu	Cnemotriccus fuscatus
Greater Ani	Anu-coroca	Crotophaga major
Green Ibis	Corocoró	Mesembrinibis cayennensis
Helmeted Woodpecker	Pica-pau-de-cara-amarela	Dryocopus galeatus
Large-tailed Antshrike	Borralhara-assobiadora	Mackenziaena leachii
Plush-crested Jay	Gralha-Picaça	Cyanocorax chrysops
Ringed Kingfisher	Martim-pescador-grande	Ceryle torquatus
River Warbler	Pula-pula-ribeirinho	Phaeothlypis rivularis
Rufous Gnateater	Chupa-dente	Conopophaga lineata
Russet-winged Spadebill	Patinho-gigante	Platyrinchus leucoryphus
Slaty-breasted Wood-rail	Saracura-do-mato	Aramides saracura
Tufted Antshrike	Brujajara	Mackenziaena severa
Wattled Jacana	Jacanã	Jacana jacana
White-bearded Manakin	Rendeira	Manacus manacus
Yellow Tyrannulet	Marianinha-amarela	Capsiempis flaveola

MATA ATLÂNTICA: SOUTHEAST

With a much-quoted density of 450 plant species per hectare, the biodiversity of the Mata Atlântica is even greater than that of the Amazon. It has approximately 20,000 different kinds of plants. Around half of the tree species and 80% of the primates are endemic. It harbours an estimated 250 species of mammals, 340 of amphibians and 1020 of birds.
Sadly, it also holds the record for endangered species. In its coastal, and unique, *restinga* forests there are several species threatened with extinction.

All of the southeastern Mata Atlântica parks, close as they are to places like Rio and São Paulo, have excellent infrastructure and are easily reached. If you travel to Rio, you don't even have to leave the city to go to the Tijuca National Park.

Threatened Species

Pectoral Antwren
Neotropical Otter
Maldonado Red-bellied Toad
Golden Frog
Slender Mouse Opossum
Woolly Spider Monkey
Golden Lion Tamarin

Opposite, top to bottom:
A Green-headed Tanager;
Upper Itatiaia cabeça-do-negro
grass; A brown-throated sloth
with a baby clinging to her.

Mata Atlântica: Southeast

Park Statistics

Area: 300km² (116 sq miles).
Rainfall: There is a vast variation depending on the month and the altitude. Generally between 1250 (49 in) and 1500mm (59 in) annually.
Temperature: In Lower Itatiaia, temperature averages 20–22°C (68–71°F), with the coldest month being July (4°C/39°F) and the hottest January when it can reach 36°C (97°F). In Upper Itatiaia alpine temperatures prevail.
Opening times: Lower Itatiaia – open daily, 08:00–17:00. Entry R$3 per person, $5 per car, $10 per minibus. There is a paved road inside the park. Upper Itatiaia – open daily 07:00–14:00, gate manned and open until 17:00. Entry R$12 per person.

Parque Nacional do Itatiaia

Itatiaia was Brazil's first national park. It was created on 14 June 1937 and is located on the Mantiqueira mountain range, in southwestern Rio de Janeiro state crossing into the state of Minas Gerais. For once the clichéd label 'ruggedly beautiful' means what it says: though only 100-odd kilometres (62-odd miles) from the Atlantic Ocean, its altitude varies from 700m to 2500-plus and it includes the Pico das Prateleiras at 2548m (8360ft) and the Pico das Agulhas Negras which, at 2791.5m (9159ft), new official height, measured by GSM, is the fifth highest peak in Brazil. Itatiaia's name means 'many sharp peaks' in Tupi-Guarani, referring to the broken-comb-like granite cliffs of Agulhas Negras, which in turn mean 'Black Needles' in Portuguese.

Even before it was designated a national park, thus kick-starting Brazil's eco-protection journey that continues to this day, it was the site of a biological research station that was part of Rio's Botanical Gardens, which is still very much active in projects in the area. Its aim was to try and cultivate fruit normally grown in temperate zones, a plan that ended in failure; but it was this failure that resulted in the creation of the park.

Itatiaia made headlines in June 1985 when a snowstorm – a rare event in Brazil – stunned and stranded hikers, tourists and rangers for nine hours with wind-chill-factor temperatures plummeting to the decidedly un-Brazilian -13°C (8.6°F) at the highest elevations, with 1m (0.6 in) of snow accumulating on the ground. (This is not the coldest temperature measured in Brazil, however; the record is held since 1952 by the city of Caçador in Santa Catarina: -14°C, without the help of the wind.) It made headlines again in 2007 when the film *Itatiaia, A Look From Inside* by Christian Spencer and Gibby Zobel won the Special Award of the International Jury in the 33rd Ekofilm International Film Festival in the Czech Republic.

The park is divided into two. Lower Itatiaia (up to 1500m/ 4921ft) has both primary and secondary Atlantic rainforest, lakes, rivers and waterfalls such as the famous Véu da Noiva (Bride's Veil) that stretches 30m (98ft) up the Maromba ravine. There are numerous hiking trails that start from the Visitors'

Parque Nacional do Itatiaia

Centre and can be reached by car or by regular bus from the village of Itatiaia. There is a wide spectrum of tropical flora that ranges from hardwoods such as *ipé* trees (*Tabebuia sp.*); two species of Jequitibás, the White (*Cariniana legalis*) and the Red (*Cariniana estrellensis*), which are gigantic trees that reach 60m (197ft) in height and live for 3000 years; humble glorybushes and Asparagus Ferns (*Asparagus setaceus*) as well as orchids, lianas, cacti, mosses, fuchsias, lilies and begonias, as every trunk and branch is utilized to support this climber or that creeper. The park gives refuge to 294 species of birds, 67 species of mammals and, rather

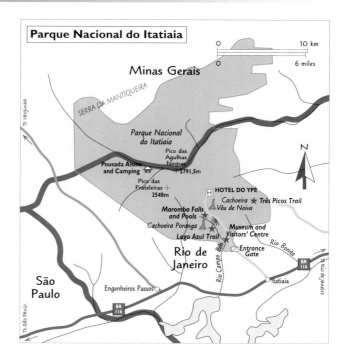

surprisingly for such elevations, 2260 species of insects and spiders, including 18 viciously biting sandflies. There are strange creatures to be seen, like the *bicho-pau* (*Phiblossoma phyllinum*), a stick insect that looks exactly like a twig, and the *bicho-folhas* (*Tanusia, Pterochroza, Mimetica* and *Typophyllum* species) that are hard to distinguish from brown, withered leaves. Mammals include pumas, squirrels, agoutis, coatis and tapirs as well as rare species of monkeys such as the Southern Muriqui (*Brachyteles arachnoides*) and the Black-fronted Titi (*Callicebus nigrifrons*), plus the more common Black Capuchin (*Cebus nigritus*) and Brown Howler Monkey (*Alouatta guariba*).

Between 1500 and 2300m (4921 and 7546ft) of altitude there is transitional vegetation such as cloud forests. These are created when the hot, humid sea air rises up the slopes of the mountains and eventually cools to form rain or a perpetual mist that hangs foggily over the forest canopy like a cloud.

Mata Atlântica: Southeast

Accommodation

There is plenty of accommodation in the nearby villages of Itatiaia, Penedo and Visconde de Mauá, but the novelty here is to stay inside a Brazilian national park.

Hotel do Ypê: The hotel stands at the highest altitude, close to all the big waterfalls. Turn off at Park Highway Km 13. It has fantastic views and all meals are included in the price. Recommended. Tel: (24) 3352-1453, www.hoteldoype.com.br

Pousada Esmeralda: Turn off at Park Highway Km 8. Tel: (24) 3352-1643, www.pousadaesmeralda.com.br

Hotel Donati: Turn off at Park Highway Km 11. Tel: (24) 3352-1509, www.hoteldonati.com.br

Vista Linda: A hotel with amazing views. Turn off at Park Highway Km 4. Tel: (24) 3352-1124, www.vistalindahotel.com.br

Chalés Terra Nova: Turn-off at Park Highway Km 4.5. Tel: (24) 3352-1458, www.chalesterranova.com.br

As it takes two hours to drive from the Lower Itatiaia to the entrance of Upper Itatiaia you may want to stay nearer the upper gate at **Pousada** and **Camping Alsine**, and **Pousada dos Lobos**. Just by the turn off to the park, there is the **Pousada São Conrado** at Garganta do Registro.

In the less well-travelled Upper Itatiaia that encompasses 14% of the park and stands above 2300m (7546ft), there are the less-trodden grassy meadows of the Altitude Fields and the hikes to the peaks. The vegetation here is surprisingly similar to the Andean on the other side of the continent, with the main grasses being the *cabeça-do-negro* (*Cortaderia modesta*) which can be distinguished from the thinner (*Cladium encipholium*) by its orange tip; the Brazilian bamboo *Chusquea pinifolia*, a dwarf compared with the oriental variety; and the bromeliad-like *Actinocephalus pholiantus*.

This is an all-round park offering peaceful hikes in Lower Itatiaia that can be enjoyed by families, and mountaineering slopes in Upper Itatiaia for extreme sports enthusiasts.

Best time to go

The best time to climb the mountain peaks is during the cold, dry season between June and September. The best hiking time in Lower Itatiaia is in September and October when it is a bit warmer and wetter, but before the onset of the big rains.

How to get there

The Dutra Highway BR-116 between São Paulo and Rio de Janeiro passes by the village of Itatiaia which is 5km (3 miles) away from the park boundary. There are regular buses to and from São Paulo and Rio de Janeiro.

To climb the two main peaks you must arrive at the Upper Visitors' Entrance, reached off the Dutra Highway via the exit (330 or 330a depending on whether you are driving from Rio or São Paulo) on the BR-354 through Engenheiro Passos. The turn-off from the BR-354 to the Upper Itatiaia entrance is at Itamonte at the frontier with Minas Gerais. It involves 17km (10.5 miles) of unpaved road to reach Ponto 3, where you pay the entrance fee, and the ultimate station, Abrigo Rebouças, where you disembark for the hike. This is the highest road in Brazil, and possibly the worst. (It is not recommended to drive your own or any rented car there, even if it is a 4WD; opt instead for one of the guides' jeeps). After that, the trail to the right leads to Prateleiras and the one to the left to Agulhas Negras. Only hikes with an authorized IBAMA guide are allowed.

Parque Nacional do Itatiaia

What to see
Lower Itatiaia
You can choose several trails or drives passing by or leading to the park's main attractions. In increasing distance from the entrance gate:

Ultimo Adeus Vista: Two kilometres (1 mile) from the entrance, accessible by car, this is a panoramic view over the valley of the Rio Campo Belo; even the Furnas hydroelectric station on the south side fits in perfectly with the artificial reservoir it has created. The Rio Campo Belo along with the Rio Bonito traverse the park, producing several pools and waterfalls, but it is the former that is the heart and soul of the park, starting as a small spring in Upper Itatiaia by the side of the trail to Agulhas Negras.

The Museum in the Visitors' Centre should be an obligatory stop so that you can familiarize yourself with the park's wildlife. As befits the history of the park as a biological research station, the collection of flora, fauna and geological samples is substantial and its presentation scientific and systematic.

Lago Azul Trail: This is a short circuit to a deep blue lake formed by the Campo Belo River, the first major feature of the park, but it only gets deep during the rainy season.

Cachoeira Poranga: 'Poranga' means 'beautiful' in Tupi-Guarani and this 10m (33ft) high waterfall with its striking emerald colouration is as pretty as they make them. It comes complete with a 30m (98ft) diameter water hole for swimming.

Maromba Falls and Pool: This is another water hole formed by several 5m (16ft) cascade that is rumoured to rejuvenate every swimmer who dives into its crystal clear waters.

The above sights can be reached either on foot or by a 4WD; the ones below can only be reached on foot.

Três Picos: This is an easy 12km (7-mile) trail to 1662m (5453ft) and a view east of the hilly landscape towards the nearby Serra da

Mata Atlântica: Southeast

Mantiqueira, the Bonito River and its waterfall. It is on this trail that trap cameras have caught pumas at night and where regular sightings of the rare southern muriqui have been made.

Cachoeira Véu de Noiva: This is the picture postcard of the Park; the Bride's Veil, a 40m (131ft) high waterfall reached via a 10km (6-mile) trail.

Upper Itatiaia

Agulhas Negras Peak: The trek to the top lasts three to four hours and is of medium difficulty but unmissable in terms of views and natural beauty. Even if you don't climb the peak, it is worth walking the flat two-hour trail to the base of the rocks to get a feel of an Andean landscape a few hours away from Rio de Janeiro.

Massif and Prateleiras Peak: Although lower at 2548m (8360ft), the climb is a much more difficult proposition than Agulhas Negras and should be undertaken only by people with a good level of fitness. Just short of the top, climbers have to jump across a crevice called 'The Cat's Leap'. Those who succeed are rewarded with a striking view over the Paraíba valley. Those who don't, need hospitalization.

Below: Upper Itatiaia Campos de Altitude landscape on course to Agulhas Negras.

Birds of Itatiaia

Itatiaia is the top bird-watching destination of southeastern Brazil, with aquatic species such as herons, grebes, anhingas and frigate birds; birds of prey like eagles, kestrels, caracaras, vultures, ospreys, kites and hawks; insect-eaters such as antwrens, antshrikes, vireos and flycatchers; as well as frugivores such as toucans. And it is that word again, biodiversity, that astounds. There are 13 species of woodpecker, 26 species of

Birds of Itatiaia

flycatcher and 20 species of tanager in the park, many of them endemic or threatened.

The birds you should expect to see are the Great Kiskadee (*Pitangus sulphuratus*) that catches insects acrobatically while flying; the Red-bellied Parakeet (*Pyrrhura frontalis*), with its long, pointed tail; the Robust Woodpecker (*Campephilus robustus*), one of the largest woodpeckers in Brazil, that announces its arrival by two knocks on a hollow tree; the Green-headed Tanager (*Tangara seledon*) whose Portuguese name (*Saíra-sete-cores*) really does justice to its seven iridescent colours; the Ruby-crowned Tanager (*Tachyphonus coronatus*) with its crown of red feathers; the Magpie Tanager (*Cissops leveriana*), largest of all tanagers, whose presence, because of its delicate nature, is an indicator of an unpolluted environment; the Red-rumped Cacique (*Cacicus haemorrhous*) with its hanging nests; the Tawny-browed Owl (*Pulsatrix koeniswaldiana*) with its *basso-profundo* cry; the Chestnut-bellied Euphonia (*Euphonia pectoralis*) that likes to mimic other birds' songs; the small, nectar-swilling Bananaquit (*Coereba flaveola*), a bird frequently confused with hummingbirds; the Dusky-legged Guan (*Penelope obscura*), an endangered species that can be easily spotted around the Visitors' Centre; the Surucuá Trogon (*Trogon surrucura*) which is a smaller relative of the Resplendent Quetzal of Central America; the Red-breasted Toucan (*Ramphastos dicolorus*); the Squirrel Cuckoo (*Piaya cayana*) that jumps about from branch to branch like a squirrel; the Blue-naped Chlorophonia (*Chlorophonia cyanea*), called *Bandeirinha* ('Little Flag') in Portuguese because its colours match those of the Brazilian flag; the Rufous-capped Motmot (*Baryphthengus ruficapillus*) that swings its long tail like a pendulum as it perches on a branch; and finally the bird that is the symbol of Brazil: the Rufous-bellied Thrush (*Turdus rufiventris*) or *sabiá-laranjeira,* whose melodic song starts off the day throughout the country.

The park is also teeming with hummingbirds such as the Black Jacobin (*Florisuga fuscus*), the Sombre Hummingbird (*Campylopterus cirrochloris*) and the Brazilian Ruby (*Clytolaema rubricauda*), while in the Higher Itatiaia there are raptors such as the Black Hawk Eagle (*Spizaetus tyrannus*) and the Roadside Hawk (*Buteo magnirostris*).

Rare Birds of the Southern Mata Atlântica

Blue-bellied Parrot
Brazilian Merganser
White-bearded Antshrike
Rio de Janeiro Antwren
Grey-winged Cotinga
Black-hooded Antwren
Buff-throated Purpletuft
Atlantic Royal Flycatcher
Three-toed Jacamar
Cherry-throated Tanager

Mata Atlântica: Southeast

Biodiversity Hotspots

Biodiversity is generally defined as the variability among all the different species of plants, animals and micro-organisms, including within-species genetic variability. Scientists estimate that the Earth's total biota (i.e. discovered plus estimated undiscovered species) consists of more than 10 million species and that less than a quarter have been identified. The greatest proportion of discovered species, around 20%, are to be found in Brazil. According to a study published in July 2005, Brazil's total biota was estimated at between 1.4 and 2.4 million. The known biota was estimated at 170,000–210,000 species, with 40,000–50,000 floral species and 100,000 to 140,000 animal species. A biodiversity hotspot is an area with a large number of endemic species. Conservation International has nominated 34 such hotspots worldwide (covering just 2.3% of the earth's surface area) where three-quarters of the planet's most threatened mammals, birds, and amphibians survive. Brazil's contribution to the global hotspots are the Mata Atlântica and the Cerrado.

Brazil's endangered monkeys

Because of extensive habitat destruction, six out of Brazil's seven critically endangered species are monkeys that are endemic to the Mata Atlântica: Golden-rumped Lion Tamarin (*Leontopithecus chrysopygus*), Coimbra's Titi (*Callicebus coimbrai*), the Northern Bahian Blond Titi (*Callicebus barbarabrownae*), the Northern Muriqui (*Brachyteles hypoxanthus*), the Buffy-headed Capuchin (*Cebus xanthosternos*) and the Black-faced Lion Tamarin (*Leontopithecus caissara*). The Brazilian Arboreal Mouse (*Rhagomys rufescens*), a rodent, completes the list.

But it is the endangered and strikingly good-looking Golden Lion Tamarins (*Leontopitheacus rosalia*) that have captured the imagination of conservationists worldwide. Only 30cm (12in) long, excluding their 40cm (16in) tails, with a golden-orange mane forming a 360-degree hairy halo around their heads and a brown expressive face, they have become the poster-boys of the movement. European and North American resources were poured into the ecological reserves in Brazil where an intensive breeding programme has met with unqualified success. In 1980, fewer than 100 individuals remained in the wild; by 1990 the number had increased to 450, even excluding animals re-introduced from captive stock. By now the wild population is well into four figures and rising, and there are about 500 animals kept in captivity. A higher percentage of lion tamarins born in the wild survives in the rainforest than their re-introduced parents, which suggests that the long-term prospects look good.

The behaviour of the lion tamarins themselves helped their continued existence. They live in reproductive groups averaging six individuals that occupy stable territories normally consisting of two breeding adults and younger animals. The group co-operates by helping each other, carrying and feeding the young, warning each other against predators and protecting the territory against other groups. Thus, releasing a group together improves the survival prospects of all of its members, as family integrity is maintained and the resulting communal defence mechanisms kick in.

Golden lion tamarins need a high forest canopy with dense tangles of vines so that they can evade predators such as raptors,

Brazil's endangered monkeys

large cats and snakes. The canopy also provides them with food (insects and fruit), drink (rainwater caught in bromeliads) and shelter (they sleep in abandoned nests or tree holes). The destruction of the Atlantic rainforest means that they are now concentrated in 18 different isolated patches, so it is unlikely that these animals will ever again roam Rio de Janeiro's Mata Atlântica, but they are slowly but surely moving out of danger of extinction.

The muriqui – one of the world's rarest mammals – has not been as lucky as the lion tamarin. Two distinct species are now recognized whose ranges do not overlap: the Southern Muriqui (*Brachyteles arachnoides*) that lives in the forests of the states of São Paulo, Rio de Janeiro and Paraná (including the park of Itatiaia), and the Northern Muriqui (*Brachyteles hypoxanthus*) that lives in the states of Minas Gerais, Espírito Santo and Bahia.

Below: Antonio Pigafetta, Magellan's own scribe on board, described the golden lion tamarins as 'beautiful, simian-like cats, similar to small lions'.

Maybe muriquis have suffered this fate because they are less photogenic than lion tamarins: their fur is a drab grey-brown and their bodies look far too bulky for their long, gangly arms and legs. Maybe it is because they live in larger groups of up to 40 individuals that are not territorial and as a result are much less aggressive and competitive than lion tamarins. Or maybe it is their breeding behaviour: the female gives birth to a single baby during the dry season whereas a lion tamarin female normally gives birth to twins twice a year. Whatever the reasons, the muriqui population has decreased from an estimated 400,000 when Brazil was first 'discovered' down to less than 1000 Southern and less than 300 Northern Muriquis in 2003.

South American Bigfoot?

The *guayazi*, the *didi* and the *vasitri* ('big devil') are the South American Indian

Mata Atlântica: Southeast

versions of the North American Bigfoot and the Tibetan yeti: large ape-like creatures that supposedly attack women and, like the *boto* dolphin, cause unwanted pregnancies. Interestingly, part of a femur and a humerus of an ape-like creature, named *Protopithecus brasiliensis*, had been discovered in Brazil by the Danish naturalist, Peter W. Lund back in 1836, but 19th-century discoverers refused to believe him. This was, after all, the continent where its largest river had been named after an encounter with a fabled women-only warrior tribe.

A photograph of a strange creature shot in Sierra de Perijaa on the Venezuelan–Colombian border by the Swiss adventurer, Dr Francois de Loys, re-ignited the issue in the 1920s. A French anthropologist, Georges Montandon, took up the story that was eventually published in the *Illustrated London News* and created a stir in the French Academy of Sciences. There was a heated debate at the time about the existence or not of a South American gorilla or even an anthropoid missing link but, with only a photograph as evidence, Montandon's thesis was eventually defeated.

But rarely is there smoke without fire. In 1992, a complete skeleton of what has since been identified as the same species *Protopithecus brasiliensis,* was discovered in the Toca da Boa Vista cave in Bahia. Although the animal was hardly gigantic – it only weighed about 25kg (55 lb) – it was still twice the weight of the largest monkey alive in South America today. So, in line with sloths, armadillos and capybaras, there have been giant Neotropical monkeys who were considerably larger than their current descendants. But let us qualify that term 'giant': they were still below the size of an adult chimpanzee or gorilla – let alone the bulk of the legendary Bigfoot.

Park Statistics

Area: 33km² (12 sq miles), the second smallest national park in Brazil, only larger than the Marine Park of Fernando de Noronha. **Rainfall:** Between 1250mm (49 in) and 1500mm (59 in) annually. **Temperature:** Average 22–24°C (68–71°F), reaching 38°C (100°F) in the summer and 4°C (39°F) at night in the winter.

Parque Nacional da Tijuca

Maybe this national park is not an attraction in itself, but an added bonus to the 'marvellous city' of Rio de Janeiro wherein it lies. The Lagoa Rodrigo de Freitas (right in the middle of the Zona Sul) and the Corcovado hill (with the statue of Christ the Redeemer) are both in theory parts of the park, which means that it receives more than 700,000 visitors annually. It has the

Parque Nacional da Tijuca

luxury not only of paved roads, but paved trails and bicycle paths, car parks, top restaurants, picnic sites, a train that climbs up the Corcovado, a helipad on the Vista Dona Maria, designer lookouts like the Vista Chinesa pavilion, hang-gliding off Bonita Rock, plus possibilities for abseiling and mountaineering.

The most remarkable thing about Tijuca, though, is that it exists at all. The whole park is replanted secondary – though native – forest. It was the first regenerated wilderness in South America, a fact that is rendered even more impressive when one learns that private, commercial coffee plantations were appropriated to establish the park. That this was allowed to happen was because the project's instigator, Brazil's Emperor Pedro II, was an absolute monarch, untempered by a parliament.

Above: *A view of Lagoa and Ipanema from Corcovado inside the Tijuca National Park.*

Yet it worked. The forest of Tijuca was created in 1862 and 100,000 seedlings were planted over 13 years, followed by 30,000 more between 1875 and 1887. By the end of the 19th century, the reforestation was complete and the place is now indistinguishable from any of the nearby primary Mata Atlântica reserves. The woods include Angicos (*Piptadenia sp.*), Pink and Silver Trumpet trees (*Tabebuia sp.*), Queen (*Syagrus romanzoffianum*) and Juçara Palms (*Euterpe edulis*), Evergreen Quebrachos (*Schinopsis sp.*), Jequitibás (*Cariniana estrellensis*), Sapucaias (*Lecythis ollaria*) and Sibipirunas (*Caesalpinia peltophoroides*). There are many interesting and unique trees, such as the Pau-jacaré or Caiman trees (*Piptadenia gonoacantha*) which have a series of thorns when young which, when older, merge to form sharp ridges like the skin of a crocodile; Jabuticabas (*Myrciaria cauliflora*) on whose fruit the coati lives on; tall Jequitibas (*Cariniana legalis*) that rise to 30m (98ft); Ingás (*Inga sp.*), whose fruit is highly prized by the capuchin monkeys; and finally Embaubas (*Cecropia palmata*), whose leaves feed the

Limerick
County Library

Mata Atlântica: Southeast

sloths and whose hollow bark is used by ants to make their home in. Unfortunately, some non-native trees such as eucalyptus were also planted and two have become veritable pests: dracaenas from Africa (*Dracaena sp.*) and Jackfruit (*Artocarpus heterophyllus*) from Malaysia.

In the remote parts of Tijuca there are tapirs and giant otters, pumas and maned wolves, boas and anacondas, as well as peccaries and giant anteaters. In the more trodden paths, you can meet coatis, capuchin monkeys, crab-eating foxes, sloths, opossums and armadillos, while toucans, hawks, tanagers, parrots, wood rails, doves and hummingbirds are readily seen. Some bird species to look out for are the Red-shouldered or Maracanã Macaw (*Diopsittaca nobilis*) that has given its name to the famous Brazilian football stadium (the joke goes that the crowd cries as wildly as the parrot); the Olivaceous Woodcreeper or subideira (*Sittasomus griseicapillus*); the Plain Parakeet (*Brotogeris tirica*); the Brassy-breasted Tanager (*Tangara desmaresti*); the White-necked Jacobin (*Florisuga mellivora*), a sparkling-blue hummingbird; the White-barred Piculet (*Picumnus cirratus*) which belongs to the woodpecker family; the Black-beaked Toucan (*Ramphastos vitellinus*); the Green-headed Tanager (*Tangara seledon*); the Scaly-headed Parrot (*Pionus maximiliani*); and the Blue Manakin or tangará dançador (*Chiroxiphia caudata*), whose males dance in threes for a female on a branch, like the cock-of-the-rock to whom they are related. A raptor that is easily spotted around the Visitors' Centre is the grey Mantled Hawk (*Leucopternis polionotus*).

There are many morpho butterflies here, including the White Morpho (*Morpho polyphemus*) and the scintillating Capitão-do-Mato (*Morpho achilles achillaena*). On a more sombre note, there is a tiny spider, the yellow-and-black Aranha-armadeira (*Phoneutria nigriventer*) – more venomous than a tarantula – that turns its belly up when it sees you and jumps on you if you decide to approach. There are also thousands of poisonous jararacas or Neuwieds Lanceheads (*Bothrops neuwiedi*) and Uruguayan Coral Snakes (*Micrurus altirostris*) outside the trails. And there are plenty of the latter; the park guide lists 90 trails in all with a total length of 70km (43 miles).

Parque Nacional da Tijuca

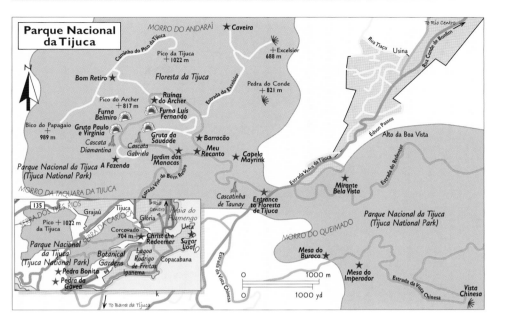

Best time to go

The best time to go is from March to September when it is drier.
During December to February it is peak season and all the
'Cariocas' (inhabitants of Rio de Janeiro) dash to the park.

How to get there

The park is criss-crossed by roads and has seven points of access
in seven different entrances: Sumare (Rua Sumare), Caixa D'agua
dos Caboclos (Rua Almirante Alexandrino), Macacos (Rua Dona
Castorina), Passo de Pedras (Rua Vista Chinesa), Sapucaias (Rua
do Redentor), Solidão (Rua Acude da Solidão – exit only), and
Cascatinha (Rua da Cascatinha). It is open daily from 08:00–17:00.

What to see

The park is divided in four sectors and is crossed by highways
(and mined under by the Rebouças Tunnel). The Estrada das
Canoas reaches the coastal part (Sector C) looking over the
beach of São Conrado; Sector B is the most frequented and
visible part of the park and includes Corcovado; finally, the

Mata Atlântica: Southeast

As Tijuca is inside Rio city limits, the full gamut of accommodation in Rio is on offer. However, if you want to be close to the Tijuca National Park, consider:

Hotel InterContinental Rio: by Pedra da Gávea and near the Gávea Golf Club, Av. Prefeito Mendes de Morais 222, São Conrado, tel: (21) 3323 2200, www.ichotelsgroup.com/h/d/ic/1/en/hd/RIOHA

Hotel Promenade Paradiso: at the end of the Floresta da Tijuca road, Av. das Américas 487, Barra da Tijuca. Reservations through call centre, tel: (31) 2125-3540, www.promenade.com.br

Many people consider a self-contained flat much more convenient, especially if they stay for at least a week.

Rent Apart: self-contained flats in the up-market districts of Gávea/Jardim Botanico/Leblon/Ipanema, tel: (21) 9156-2245/(21) 2511-2053, www.rentapart.com.br/index_ing.htm

Avenida Edson Passos/Estrada das Furnas divides Sector B from Sector A, which is called Floresta da Tijuca and contains the two main climbing peaks: Tijuca and Papagaio. There is also sector D (Covanca/Pretos Forros) that is a continuation of Sector C, but is closed to the public and used for research purposes.

Coastal trails

In Sector C, you can access the photogenic rocks of Pedra da Gávea and Pedra Bonita, looking over Rio's Atlantic beaches, via six different easy hikes measuring around 5.1km (3 miles). These are: the Bonita trail (1340m/4396ft to altitude 696m/2283ft), which leads to the easy Chapecó trail (320m/1050ft to altitude 554m/1817ft) with a beautiful panoramic point at the end. The Escorrega trail (530m/1739ft to altitude 696m/2283ft) merges with the Agulhinha trail (345m/1132 to altitude 610m/2001ft). The Pedra da Gávea trail is only 1670m (5479ft) long but it is classified as hard: it takes three hours to reach an altitude of 530m (1739ft). Finally, the Pedra Bonita trail (1000m/3281ft to altitude 550m/1804ft) reaches a hang-gliding platform; from there, another short and steep 70m (230ft) path at 15 degrees incline leads to a higher point (550m/1804ft), also used for hang-gliding.

Cariocas mountain range

Here the best-regarded hike is the two-hour difficult climb to Corcovado that starts inside Lage Park by the School of Visual Arts and meanders gently around a stream with two small waterfalls. It gets seriously difficult after the second waterfall, until it reaches the Corcovado rail line at the panoramic point, appropriately called 'Vista of Oh'. From there onwards the road is asphalted and you reach the top and the statue of Christ at 704m (2310ft). Note that there have been some muggings recently on this trail and you are advised not to attempt the climb alone. A safer proposition is to drive up the Corcovado to the entrance of the train to the top and continue by car on the single winding road, stopping at the many panoramic points to admire the view, and exit from the other side.

Floresta da Tijuca

This is the main part of the park and the wildest. Before the advent of GPS, hikers who strayed from the paths used to get lost

Parque Nacional da Tijuca

Left: Forest surrounding Christ the Redeemer statue, one of the most popular sights in Rio de Janeiro.

just like in a proper rainforest. Although the last such case occurred in 1999, it is easy to see why as you make your way through the thick vegetation and mobile reception disappears. There are asphalted roads through the park, with the best drive of all from the Cascatinha entry to the panoramas of Excelsior and Bom Retiro, leaving through the Açude da Solidão exit. The four-hour Cachoeira das Almas circuit shadows this drive, but it is well away from the road itself and is best undertaken with a guide as it passes through very dense secondary vegetation.

The most popular hikes are to the peaks. The medium-difficult two-hour Tijuca climb (2.6km/1.6 miles) starts from the Bom Retiro car park (661m/2169ft) and continues with a possible side-excursion to the smaller Tijuca Mirim (917m/3008ft) halfway, before the final climb up the Tijuca peak itself (1022m/3353ft). It is possible to connect with the Andaraí Maior (861m) trail and end by the old Caveira farm (three to four hours in all). The northwestern side has the more challenging and less well-travelled hikes but is also more likely to contain interesting wildlife. These are the three to four hour trail (2.3km/1.4 miles) to the Bico de Papagaio (Parrot's Beak, 989m/3245ft), possibly returning via the Morro da Cocanha (982m/3221ft, 2.4km/1.3 miles) to the Solidão exit. All these hikes start at Bom Retiro car park where there are also facilities, guards to look after your car but no mobile reception, so if you arrange for a taxi, you have to name a fixed hour for it to pick you up.

Nearby attractions are numerous, and involve the whole of the city of Rio de Janeiro, but one site that many visitors to Rio miss out on is the Botanical Gardens in Leblon. They were created by Dom Pedro II's grandfather, Dom João VI, king of Portugal, in 1822 after he fled to Brazil during the Napoleonic wars. They contain 7000 native plants (including a *pau-brasil* tree) arranged in areas representative of Brazil's biomes, and have been extended to contain oriental species and plants, including a Japanese garden. For anyone who is interested in Brazil's natural history the Botanical Gardens are a must.

Below: The slow movements of the sloths help them retain their low metabolism.

Tree sloths

Nothing in the jungle moves as slowly as the sloths. They spend so much of their time hanging upside down from the branches (where they eat fruit and munch leaves and twigs) that grooves on their fur – which grows in the reverse direction than that of any other mammal to allow water to dribble off – are home to infestations of greenish algae. This is an advantage in the jungle, because it allows sloths to camouflage themselves well among the trees. Their head has also adapted well to life upside down and can turn 270 degrees. Surprisingly, for such a slow-moving arboreal animals they are also excellent swimmers.

There are only five species of sloth today belonging to two genera, depending on the number of front toes that are armed with hook-like claws: the two-toed (*Choloepus sp.*) and three-toed sloths (*Bradypous sp.*). They both belong to an ancient order originating in the Late Eocene epoch about

The Bush Dog

35 million years ago, which also contained some gigantic, land-based species such as the giant *Megatherium,* which was as big as an elephant. Its descendants today are much smaller: about 60–80cm (23–31 in) in length, they can weigh 8–9kg (18–20 lb). The reason for their long survival is their low metabolism. Their slow movements purely serve to conserve energy; they would hardly have been able to sustain a body of their mass otherwise.

The only reason sloths descend to the ground – and forest animals and sloth-watchers must be grateful for this act of civility – is to defecate, a once-a-week event. Unlike the anteaters and armadillos to which they are related, sloths' sharp, curved claws do not allow them to walk in their ground, so whenever they find themselves there they crawl on their bellies and pull themselves forward. They also mate in the trees and the male disappears afterwards leaving the female to give birth to a single baby after an unsurprisingly long gestation of nine months. The baby hangs from its mother's hair, bleating like a sheep if it is separated, until it is weaned.

The Bush Dog

The Bush Dog (*Speothos venaticus*) is a strange animal, the only remaining species of a prehistoric extinct canine family whose remains have been found in the Lagoa Santa caves of Brazil. Scientists have been baffled as regards its taxonomy; some put it in the same branch as the African wild dog, others insist it is a cousin of the Crab-eating Fox (*Cerdocyon thous*), which, despite its name and its appearance, is another Neotropical canid. However, recent DNA analysis makes it a distant relative of the Maned Wolf (*Chrysocyon brachyurus*), which is baffling, for the two species could not look more different.

Unlike the fox-on-stilts appearance of the tall, slender, maned wolf, the bush dog is short (20cm/8 in on the shoulder) and elongated like a dachshund (60–70cm/23–28 in) with a head, muzzle and fur like a ferret's and webbed feet like an otter's. Its Brazilian name (*cachorro-vinagre* or vinegar-dog) describes its striking tawny colouration. It occurs naturally from rainforests to the southern grasslands, following the distribution of pacas which are its main source of food. Bush dogs are formidable hunters running in packs and can occasionally take on significantly larger

Morphidae

The family Morphidae contains about 80 species that are found only in Central and South America. They include some of the most attractive groups of butterflies on the planet; the name 'Morpho' means 'beautiful'. Their wingspans range from 75–150mm (3–6 in), and the tips of their wings contain eye-like defensive camouflage markings, called ocelli. The wings are tinted iridescent blue, cyan or brown and can often change colour depending on the viewing angle. Some species have wings so thin that they appear translucent with only the ocelli showing through, a spectacle as striking as it is spellbinding.

Mata Atlântica: Southeast

Birds Translated

English name	Brazilian name	Scientific name
Bananaquit	Cambacica	Coereba flaveola
Black Jacobin	Beija-flor-preto	Florisuga fuscus
Black-beaked Toucan	Tucano-de-bico-preto	Ramphastos vitellinus
Blue-bellied Parrot	Sabiá-cica	Triclaria malachitacea
Blue-naped Chlorophonia	Bonito-do-campo or bandeirinha	Chlorophonia cyanea
Brassy-breasted Tanager	Saíra-lagarta	Tangara desmaresti
Brazilian Ruby	Beija-flor-rubi	Clytolaema rubricauda
Cherry-throated Tanager	Saíra-apunhalada	Nemosia rourei
Chestnut-bellied Euphonia	Ferro-velho	Euphonia pectoralis
Dusky-legged Guan	Jacuguaçu	Penelope obscura
Festive Coquette	Topetinho-verde	Lophornis chalybeus
Fork-tailed Flycatcher	Tesourinha	Tyrannus savana
Gray-hooded Attila	Capitão-de-saíra	Attila rufus
Great Kiskadee	Bem-te-vi	Pitangus sulphuratus
Green-headed Tanager	Saíra-de-setes-cores	Tangara seledon
Grey-winged Cotinga	Saudade-de-asa-cinza	Tijuca condita
Itatiaia Thistletail	Garrincha-chorona	Oreophylax moreirae
Magpie Tanager	Tiê-tinga	Cissops leveriana
Maracanã Macaw	Maracanã-nobre	Diopsittaca nobilis
Olivaceous Woodcreeper	Arapaçu-verde	Sittasomus griseicapillus
Orange-headed Tanager	Saíra-canário	Thlypopsis sordida
Plain Antvireo	Choquinha-lisa	Dysithamnus mentalis
Plain Parakeet	Periquito-verde	Brotogeris tirica
Red-bellied Parakeet	Tiriba-de-testa-vermelha	Pyrrhura frontalis
Red-breasted Toucan	Tucano-de-bico-verde	Ramphastos dicolorus
Red-rumped Cacique	Guaxe	Cacicus haemorrhous
Rio de Janeiro Antwren	Choquinha-fluminense	Myrmotherula fluminensis
Roadside Hawk	Gavião-carijó	Buteo magnirostris
Robust Woodpecker	Pica-pau-rei	Campephilus robustus
Ruby-crowned Tanager	Tiê-Preto	Tachyphonus coronatus
Rufous-bellied Thrush	Sabiá-laranjeira	Turdus rufiventris
Rufous-capped Motmot	Juruva-verde	Baryphthengus ruficapillus
Saffron Toucanet	Araçari-banana	Baillonius bailloni
Scaled Woodcreeper	Arapaçu-escamado	Lepidocolaptes squamatus

The Bush Dog

prey such as capybaras, rheas or even deer by attacking their legs until the animals get tired and drop to the ground from exhaustion. Indigenous people have traditionally kept bush dogs as pets and use them to flush out prey like agoutis or armadillos from burrows in the same way as bloodhounds are used during the fox hunt.

The bush dog is one of the few social carnivorous land mammals in South America and forms packs of 2–12 individuals that communicate with each other through a gamut of barks. The pack is a monogamous family unit, with offspring living with their parents until they are mature enough to breed. When they do, the male shares the rearing of the young and provides the female with food while she is pregnant or nursing the pups.

Above: *Packs of bush dogs are such good hunters that native Amerindians used to follow their barks to steal their prey.*

Birds Translated

English name	Brazilian name	Scientific name
Slaty-breasted Wood-rail,	Saracura-do-mato	*Aramides saracura*
Sombre Hummingbird	Beija-flor-cinza	*Campylopterus cirrochloris*
Squirrel Cuckoo	Alma-de-gato	*Piaya cayana*
Star-throated Antwren	Choquinha-de-garganta-pintada	*Myrmotherula gularis*
Streamer-tailed Tyrant	Tesoura-do-brejo	*Gubernetes yetapa*
Surucuá Trogon	Surucuá-de-barriga-vermelha	*Trogon surrucura*
Tawny-browed Owl	Murucututu-de-barriga-amarela	*Pulsatrix koeniswaldiana*
Versicolored Emerald	Beija-flor-de-banda-branca	*Agyrtria versicolor*
Vinaceous Parrot	Papagaio-de-peito-roxo	*Amazona vinacea*
Violet-capped Woodnymph	Beija-flor-de-fronte-violeta	*Thalurania glaucopis*
White-barred Piculet	Pica-pau-anão-barrado	*Picumnus cirratus*
White-bearded Antshrike	Chocão-de-bigode	*Biatas nigropectus*
White-bibbed Antbird	Papa-formigas-de-grota	*Myrmeciza loricata*
White-collared Foliage-gleaner	Trepador-de-coleira-branca	*Anabazenops fuscus*
White-necked Jacobin	Beija-flor-azul-de-rabo-branco	*Florisuga mellivora*

PINHERÁIS AND CAMPOS

A nyone lucky enough to be travelling on the coast of Paraná or Santa Catarina will have to try very hard to miss the tall, sturdy, *araucaria* (*Paraná pine*) forests that engarland the seaboard and define the Pinheráis ecosystem. Similarly, anyone who has travelled to the centre-west Missões region of the state of Rio Grande do Sul or reached the borders with Uruguay and Argentina will have witnessed the change of the landscape into the grassy rolling hills that make up Campos. These two small Brazilian biomes do not have distinct national parks or reserves that serve to illustrate their ecosystems except maybe Paraná's Marumbi State Park that runs between the state capital Curitiba and the coast, which offers more than a glimpse of those handsome pines.

Rare Birds

Speckled Crake
Solitary Tinamou
Yellow-legged Tinamou
Rufous-thighed Kite
White-rumped Hawk
Black-and-white Hawk Eagle
Red-and-white Crake
South American Painted-Snipe
Pheasant Cuckoo

Opposite, top to bottom:
Despite its name, the majority of the crab-eating fox's diet is composed of small vertebrates and fruit.; a Brazilian tapir swimming; pampas deers.

Pinheráis and Campos

Park Statistics

Area: 131km² (51 sq miles). For all intents and purposes, Aparados da Serra forms one protected area with the adjoining Serra Geral National Park (which, however, has no infrastructure). The two parks are managed together.
Rainfall: It rains all year round, with an average precipitation of 1500–2250mm (59–88 in). The wettest month is September.
Temperature: Average temperature is 18–20°C (64–68°F), but it falls to below zero at night during the winter and reaches 34–36°C (93–96°F) during the summer.
Opening times: The park is open 09:00–17:00 Wednesday–Sunday. It is open on public holidays that fall on Mondays or Tuesdays but is closed on the day immediately after. Entry is R$6 per person, with children below 7 years old and seniors over 70 allowed free. There is a paying car park by the entrance (R$5 for a car, R$10 for a bus). The nearby park of Serra Geral is open daily 08:00–18:00 and entry is free.

Parque Nacional Aparados da Serra

The major park in the area, Aparados da Serra, although strictly speaking residing within the Mata Atlântica, contains a mixture of all three biomes that border its boundaries: southern Mata Atlântica montane cloud forest (called *matinha nebular* here); coastal forest with 25m (82ft) tall Cangerana (*Cabralea cangerana*) and Maria-Mole trees (*Guapira nitida*); high montane conifer forests typical of Pinheráis with Araucaria trees (*Araucaria angustifolia*), Pinheiros-bravos, (*Podocarpus lambertii*) or holly bushes called *caúnas* (*Ilex theezans*); and Campos grasslands. It is indicative of the difficulty of preserving such pristine environments that the issue of land tenure is still in dispute over one-third of its area. Cattle ranches, domestic pets, non-native tree cultivation and banana plantations impinge destructively on the park's ecosystem.

Best time to go

Clear skies and high visibility but low temperatures prevail mostly in the winter, between May and August. Mist descends on the canyons at the end of the rainy season in March and April.

How to get there

The park straddles the border between the states of Santa Catarina and Rio Grande do Sul. It is best reached from Porto Alegre by taking the State Highway RS-020 towards São Francisco de Paula and Cambará do Sul, from where a short, unpaved road leads you

Right: The typical rolling hill landscape of Campos, Missões district.

Parque Nacional Aparados da Serra

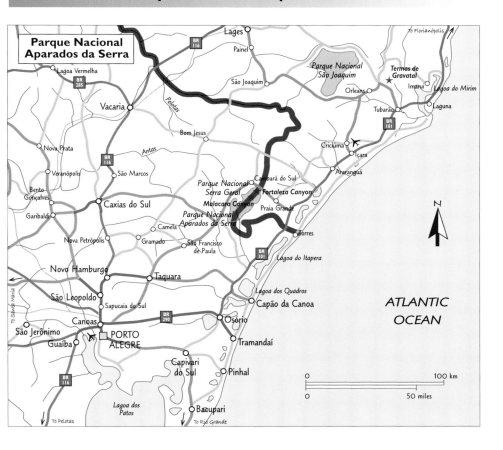

to the park. It is more difficult to reach from Santa Catarina where the BR-101 highway takes you to Praia Grande. A final winding dirt road through the Serra do Faxinal takes you to the park.

What to see

The main attraction in Aparados da Serra is the canyon of Itaimbezinho, a raw, starkly attractive gorge 5.8km (3.6 miles) long with a maximum width of 2km (1 mile) and height of 720m (2362ft). Its chalky, rocky sides, created 130 million years ago, are covered with bush and pines forming a landscape that brings to mind that of the Blue Mountains of New South Wales or the South African Escarpment. It is no surprise to learn that all three

Pinheráis and Campos

were geographically attached to each other before the big continental split, hundreds of millions of years ago.

One should add that there are more than 60 canyons in the vicinity. One of them, the Fortaleza canyon, is longer (7km/4 miles) and deeper (1117m/3665ft) than Itaimbezinho. It lies in the Serra Geral, is more difficult to get to and thus attracts fewer visitors.

Below: The howler monkey is one of the largest New World monkeys. There are currently nine recognized species, one of them being the black howler monkey.

Mammals that live in both parks include coatis, lesser anteaters, the Brazilian or Prehensile-tail Porcupine (*Coendou prehensilis*), tapirs, peccaries, sloths, opossums, many species of armadillo, Pacas (*Agouti paca*), Pampas Deer (*Ozotoceros bezoarticus*), capuchin and howler monkeys and, in the more remote parts, ocelots, pumas, Maned Wolves (*Chrysocyon brachyrus*) and Bush Dogs (*Speothos venaticus*).

The canyons are home to many endangered birds of prey that can be easily spotted in the park, such as the Crowned Eagle (*Harpyhaliaetus coronatus*) that used to roam on Brazil's coastal mountains and scrub forests, and the Black Hawk Eagle, whose Portuguese name 'gavião-prega-macaco' (monkey-eating vulture) is highly revealing as regards its diet, as well as more common ones like the King Vulture (*Sarcorhampus papa*) and the Azure Jay (*Cyanocorax caeruleus*), which is as strong a symbol of the Pinheráis region as

Parque Nacional Serra Geral

the jabiru stork is in the Pantanal. Other park birds that are easily spotted in the park include the Buff-necked Ibis (*Theristicus caudatus*) and the threatened Vinaceous Parrot (*Amazona vinacea*).

There are three trails in the park. The Vértice and Cotovelo trails are easy, and guides can be hired at the Visitors' Centre.

Parque Nacional Serra Geral

Visitors to Itaimbezinho who would enjoy a Far West atmosphere can go across to the Serra Geral National Park that borders Aparados da Serra. It is an untamed, harsh, craggy region with a pervading stillness that is evocative of the mid-western US states. The main attractions are the canyons of Malacara and Fortaleza which are even more remote than Itaimbezinho. A guide and GPS are recommended and IBAMA permission may be required. Opening hours are 08:00–17:00.

The three-hour medium-to-difficult trail to the canyon of Fortaleza starts at the park gate and ascends quickly and steeply to its highest point at an altitude of 1117m (3665ft) with a fantastic view of the surroundings. The walk after that is more gentle and passes by the Fortaleza waterfall halfway through.

The Malacara trail goes through the canyon of the same name and starts 6km (4 miles) from Praia Grande, by the Ecological Station Pedra Afiada. This is a three-hour medium walk and requires a guide who will show you the best way to wend your way through the stony riverbed of the Rio Malacara. There are water holes for swimming halfway along the trail.

The canyon of Malacara itself can be reached in one day by those who are fit (22km/14 miles, five hours) but if you are going that far, try the medium-to-difficult Malacara–Churriado–Fortaleza hike that lasts three days. It requires special permission from IBAMA, which is only a formality.

Opossums

Marsupials are so intimately associated with Australia that many a traveller to Brazil expresses disbelief at the fact that there is an order endemic to the Americas. They are the members of

Walking Trails

Vértice Trail:
This is an easy track that runs for 1.4km (0.8 miles) along the edge of the canyon. It leads to the Cascade of the Andorinhas (Swallows), formed by the Rio Perdiz, that falls off the top of the cliff at 700m (2297ft) and disappears in a mist before hitting the canyon floor below. There is a second cascade, the Véu de Noiva (there are numerous cascades in Brazil that are called 'the Bride's Veil') formed by the Preá Creek.

Cotovelo Trail:
This is a very satisfying 6km (4-mile), three-hour walk by the walls of Itaimbezinho, with superb views throughout, to a special panoramic and photogenic vista point. The last time of day anyone is allowed to start walking the trail is 15:00.

Rio de Boi Trail:
This is a trail that goes through Itaimbezinho itself. It follows the bed of the River Boi whose waters have carved the canyon. It is an 8km (5-mile), seven-hour difficult hike over rocky terrain that crosses the river several times. To start the walk, you drive by car until the beginning of the trail at the IBAMA post 7km (4.3 miles) away from Praia Grande. An official guide, who can be hired in Praia Grande, is obligatory.

Pineráis and Campos

Accommodation

The closest village (population: 7000) which is normally the base for the park is **Cambará do Sul**. Camping is allowed in Aparados da Serra but not in Serra Geral. **Casa da Montanha:** Take the turn-off before the park (9.5km/6 miles unpaved road). De luxe accommodation in small rural cabins (min two nights). Tel: (54) 3504-5302 / (54) 3295-7575, www.paradorcasada montanha.com.br) **Estalagem da Colina:** Modern. Av. Getúlio Vargas 80, tel: (54) 3251-1746, www.estalagemdacolina.com.br **Pousada das Corucacas:** A real *gaúcho* (South American cowboy) environment, 1km (0.6 miles) on the BR-020 outside Cambará do Sul, exit towards Ouro Verde at Fazenda Baio Ruano. Tel: (54) 3251-1123, www.guiatelnet.com.br/ pousadacorucacas **Fazenda Pindorama:** Rua João Francisco Ritter inside the park. Also has camping area. Tel: (54) 3251-1255 / 8111-3876, www.pousadapindorama.com.br **Pousada Pôr do Sol:** Rua João Francisco Ritter 960, tel: 3251-1290/1390, www.pousadapordosol.tur.br

the opossum family (*Didelphidae*), named after the Cherokee name of the animal by Captain John Smith in Jamestown, Virginia. They are not to be confused with 'possums' that live in Australia, which were named more than 150 years later by the naturalist Joseph Banks because they looked like their American cousins. And it is those Virginia Opossums (*Didelphis virginiana*) whose renowned reaction to being cornered – they pretend they're dead – has given rise to the popular phrase 'playing possum'.

More than 60 species of opossum live in South America. In Brazil they range from the large White-eared (*Didelphis albiventris*) and Big-eared Opossums (*Didelphis aurita*) that are encountered in the south, to the tiny Cerro Neblina Slender Mouse Opossum (*Marmosops neblina*) that lives within the Pico da Neblina National Park in the Amazon.

All opossums are mostly arboreal, nocturnal and solitary. They have a hallux in their hind feet, which is a toe shaped and functioning like a human thumb. Along with their long, prehensile tails, it allows them to climb up trees and hang from branches (they sometimes climb up their own tails back to the branch). As a rule, the shorter an opossum tail, the longer that species spends on the ground.

The gerbil-sized Grey Short-tailed Opossums (*Monodelphis domestica*) are reared as pets and as lab animals for research. This is because, like humans, they are susceptible to skin cancer and because the embryos are easily accessible for experimentation, as they are hidden neither in the uterus nor inside the pouch. It is hard to imagine a marsupial with no pouch, but there are always exceptions to the exceptions in nature, and this is one. After two months' gestation, the babies are born (or, being marsupials, half-born) and are immediately attached to the female's nipples by their mouths where they remain for another two weeks. Because of their importance to science, grey short-tailed opossums are the best-studied of their family and they have had the honour of being the first marsupials to have their DNA genome sequence mapped by MIT and Harvard University.

South American rodents

South American rodents

The Prehensile-tail Porcupine, also called the Brazilian Porcupine (*Coendou prehensilis*), is a rodent with a prehensile tail. Unlike other porcupines, it is mostly arboreal and has four long, clawed toes to help it climb and grip along the branches. Like so many South American species they are shy of man, nocturnal and solitary, spending most of the day up to 10m (32ft) above ground. They are quite aggressive, sometimes trying to bite each other or spike each other with their quills. If caught, they quickly roll into a ball like hedgehogs. Their diet is exclusively vegetarian and they forage on roots, leaves, seeds, fruit and even bark from trees. Like coatis, they sometimes raid farms and cause damage to crops. After a gestation of 200 days, the female gives birth to one single young during October–November; it is covered with hair and soft spines that harden very quickly after birth.

Two remote cousins of the Brazilian porcupine that are frequently confused – just check the scientific names – are the Paca (*Agouti paca*) which is large, stocky and fluffy and looks like a spotted guinea pig, and agouti, or Common Agouti (*Dasyprocta leporina*), which has been described as 'a squirrel on steroids' .

They look similar and both share the same environments, except that the agoutis are diurnal and pacas are nocturnal. Agoutis prefer the jungle undergrowth whereas pacas prefer living near lakes and rivers where, like capybaras, they escape into the water when threatened.

Pacas are the larger of the two and they are the second-largest rodent species after the capybara: they are more than 75cm (29.5 in) long and can weigh up to 14kg (31 lb). They have coarse brown fur with four or five rows of white spots on their sides and live in burrows underground. Their diet comprises seeds, plants and, mostly, fruit. Like rabbits, their meat is flavourful and they are widely eaten in South America where locals farm them for food.

Agoutis, on the other hand, are slender, nimble animals with a glossy orange-brown fur. They can grow as large as 60cm (23 in) in length and weigh up to 6kg (13 lb). They are diurnal and can often be seen standing erect on their long, muscular hind legs to chew on their food, which is similar to the pacas'. They are the only mammalian species – and that includes pacas and humans – that can crack open the hard shells of Brazil nuts with their front teeth. They bury seeds in the ground like squirrels, although there is no strict need for that as they do not have to go through a hard winter. They thus indirectly help the dispersal of trees and other vegetation.

The agoutis' courtship ritual must be one of the weirdest in nature. In order to impress the female, the male agouti showers her with his urine and sends her into a fit of sexual frenzy. Having survived this opening gambit, she stays with her mate for life. After a gestation of around four months, the female normally gives birth to twins that are fully furred and are actively jogging about almost immediately after birth. Agoutis are excellent runners and fearless swimmers; maybe it is this athleticism and

Right: An agouti. By dispersing and burying seeds, it occupies the same ecological niche as a squirrel.

The Crab-eating Fox

stable family life that explains the fact that they can live almost 20 years, a surprisingly long life span for a rodent.

The Crab-eating Fox

The Crab-eating Fox (*Cerdocyon thous*) is another one of Darwin's winners, being the descendant of a species that has existed since the Pleistocene Epoch. It has adapted to every natural environment – from lowland and montane rainforests to the Cerrado, and from the Caatinga to the Pinheráis. It takes deforestation in its stride and adjusts its diet patterns when land is urbanized or developed for agriculture: it simply rummages through human rubbish and raids the chicken coops. This fearless adaptability to human encroachment has a downside: it is the number-one roadkill in Brazil. (The slow-moving giant anteater is number two, especially in the Cerrado, and then comes the three-banded armadillo that turns into a ball when threatened – not the best strategy to avoid a speeding car.)

The crab-eating fox will eat just about anything available: rodents, frogs, lizards, eggs, fruit, carrion and, as its name suggests, it also consumes land crabs, something that must really have surprised Linnaeus who gave it its name back in 1766. However, examination of its faeces in different locations only shows a special preference for such crabs (*Dilocarcinus sp.*) in the llanos swamps of Venezuela.

One thing it is not, though, is a fox. Like the maned wolf and the bush dog, it is more closely related to canines, although its looks are totally vulpine. Its body (around 70cm/27.5 in long) is grey-brown, its elongated face and short legs have red patches and its long 30cm (12 in) tail is bushy and black-tipped. Unlike the fox, though, its fur is not valuable to man, another Darwin hit. Nor does it live in burrows, preferring instead dense undergrowth where it makes its nest.

The crab-eating fox mates for life and the pair roam together. The female gives birth to a litter once a year, and both parents take equal share in rearing their cubs, whom they start teaching how to hunt at the age of six weeks. Although it is preyed upon widely and is hunted as a pest by man, its adaptability and wide distribution has ensured the species a status of 'least concern'.

Near the Park

The Rio Tainhas forms an 80m (262ft) wide *lajeado* (shallows) called locally 'the S-Pass' that ends up in a waterfall, a popular camping and bathing place. It is possible to cross the shallows with an SUV (and much care), depending on the advice of the rangers. A little further, there is a proper camping site with facilities (café, toilets, BBQ) by a 100m (328ft) wide lake, formed again by the Rio Tainhas, with a small island in the middle which gives it its name (the Island Pass). It is 32km (20 miles) away from Cambará do Sul and costs R$5 per person.

Snake Bites

Brazil's forests and deserts harbour many venomous snakes, including rattlers, lanceheads, vipers and coral snakes. They are all afraid of man, and in the vast majority of cases they will try to avoid you and get out of your path. Similarly, if you encounter a snake, back off slowly. However, in the rare event of being bitten by a snake:
• Do not panic.
• Do not try to suck out the poison.
• Apply a clean, dry dressing to the bitten area and keep it lower than the heart or the head.
• Go straight to a medical facility.
• Do not try to kill or capture the snake. Try to remember its colour and shape, but the health professionals will normally be able tell what kind of antivenin to apply from the wound and the symptoms.

Brazil's ungulates

The various ungulates such as tapirs, peccaries and deer are the main browsing animals in the forests and fields of Brazil – and the Americas – occupying the ecological niche of the zebras and antelopes of Africa. In this respect, the New World is much more similar to the Old: the various species of deer – the Pampas (*Ozotoceros bezoarticus*), Grey Brocket (*Mazama gouazoubira*) and Red Brocket Deer (*Mazama americana*) – are not far removed from what a German or a Scot is used to seeing, and the various kinds of peccaries are not dissimilar to European Wild Boars. In the southern United States, they are in fact confused with wild hogs (razorbacks), which are domestic pigs gone feral. One way to tell peccaries from European swine is the shape of their tusks: in European boar they are long and curved, while peccaries wear them short and straight.

There are four species of peccary and all are found in Brazil: the Collared Peccary (*Pecari tajacu*), the one living in the US; the White-lipped Peccary (*Tayassu pecari*), the one usually encountered in the jungles of the Amazon and Pantanal; the Chacoan Peccary (*Catagonus wagneri*) that roams in the Campos of Brazil and Chaco of Paraguay; and, as the scientific world found out in amazement, the Giant Peccary (*Pecari maximus*), at 1.3m (4ft) in length twice as big as any other, which was only discovered by the Dutch scientist Marc van Roosmalen in March 2003 along the Aripuana River in central Amazônia. That such a large mammal could be unknown to science is indicative of the surprises that may still be hidden in the unexplored corners of Brazil.

The most unusual ungulate must be the tapir, an animal with a tough hide and a short proboscis-like prehensile snout which is made entirely of soft tissue. There are three species, but it is the Brazilian or Lowland Tapir (*Tapirus terrestris*) that is found in Brazil and occupies every ecosystem that has good freshwater sources; it likes to dive in to cool down or even graze underwater. Being 2m (6.5ft) long and 1m (3ft) high, it is as big as a pony and weighs as much as 300kg (661.5 lb). It is solitary and only comes into contact with the opposite sex during mating. Females give birth while lying on their sides and the young are dark with white or yellow spots and stripes. They feed on their mother's milk for an unusually long time, which can be as much as

Brazil's ungulates

Left: *The collared peccary also lives in North America, where it is called 'musk hog' because of its peculiar odour.*

10 months. When alarmed, tapirs dive into the water or crash into the bushes; this is not a result of blind panic, as it seems, but a carefully thought-out strategy to get rid of predators such as a puma or a jaguar that may have attacked them from above. Tapirs eat mostly fruit, leaves and plants and are the most important dispersers of Buriti palms, one of the main trees of the Brazilian *mata ciliar*. They are tame and gentle animals but their behaviour is unpredictable and they can sometimes bite humans with dire results, not only because their bite can kill, but because, strangely, they can be carriers of the rabies virus.

Birds Translated

English name	Brazilian name	Scientific name
Azure Jay	Gralha-azul	*Cyanocorax caeruleus*
Buff-necked Ibis	Curicaca	*Theristicus caudatus*
Crowned Eagle	Águia-cinzenta	*Harpyhaliaetus coronatus*
King Vulture	Urubu-rei	*Sarcorhampus papa*

NATIONAL PARKS GUIDE

Other Brazilian National Parks

Although this book showcases the best parks and areas in Brazil for viewing and admiring its diverse wildlife in all its biomes, the country has some areas of outstanding natural beauty that no book could fail to mention. There were 62 national parks in all in the country at the end of 2007 and their number increases year by year.

For those who visit the capital, Brasília, there is a national park on the outskirts of the city: **Parque Nacional de Brasília**. It has some good examples of Cerrado vegetation and the multitude of springs and streams has endowed it with the nickname '*água mineral*'. It is a good option for those who don't have the time to visit the Parque das Emas and the Chapada dos Veadeiros and if you avoid holidays or weekends, when it gets very busy, you will find it eerily empty. There are two trails, Cristal Água (5km/3 miles) and Capivara (1.3km/0.8 miles) and the park has a good population of armadillos, capuchin monkeys, capybaras and parrots. It is open every day 08:00–16:00 and entry is R$3.

For visitors to Rio who clamour for something more exotic than Tijuca, the **Parque Nacional da Serra dos Órgãos** is competing with Itatiaia for the title of the bird-watching centre of the southeast – indeed, a recent study has placed the Serra dos Órgãos region as the most diverse in bird species of the Mata Atlântica, with 462 catalogued species of birds. It also boasts closer connections to Rio than Itatiaia: buses leave for Teresópolis every hour and the journey lasts 90 minutes. Closed on Mondays, the park is open from 08:00–17:00 (entry R$3, free for children under 10 and for seniors over 65; R$12 for hikes and R$5 for vehicles). At the Teresópolis entrance, there are three trails – Trilha Suspensa, Trilha Mozart Catão and Trilha Primavera – that can all be reached by the internal road, called Estrada da Barragem. The main hike is the crossing between Petrópolis and Teresópolis, which is 30km (19 miles) long, of medium difficulty, and usually takes three days. It is a trail of renowned beauty and dramatic scenery, with great views of the mountains and over Rio de Janeiro and Guanabara Bay. Two particular sections are popular and can be attempted individually: the track to Pedra do Sino (10km/6 miles

Reptiles Translated

Anaconda
Brazilian name: Sucuri
Scientific name: *Eunectes noctaeus*

Boa Constrictor
Brazilian name: Jibóia
Scientific name: *Boa constrictor*

Caiman Lizard
Brazilian name: Víbora
Scientific name:
Dracaena paraguayensis

Spectacled Caiman
Brazilian name: Jacaré
Scientific name: *Caiman crocodilus*

Dyeing Dart Frog
Brazilian name: Sapo amarelo e preto
Scientific name: *Dendrobates tinctorius*

Green Iguana
Brazilian name: Sinimbu
Scientific name: *Iguana iguana*

Neuwied's Lancehead
Brazilian name: jararaca
Scientific name: *Bothrops neuwiedi*

Tegu Lizard
Brazilian name: Teiú
Scientific name: *Tupinambis teguixin*

Yellow-headed Sideneck Turtle
Brazilian name: Tracajá
Scientific name: *Podocnemis unifilis*

Opposite, top to bottom:
The colourful Toco Toucan;
a tourist lodge in the Amazon;
a turtle hatchling making its
way up the beach.

National Parks Guide

Remote Parks

There are many parks in the Amazon that are either off limits or even more remote than the ones discussed here. In Amapá, at the border with French Guyana, you can find the **Parque Nacional do Cabo Orange**, the only place to see both sea and river manatees in the same region. A few hundred kilometers to the west, the **Parque Nacional Montanhas do Tumucumaque** was recently created to protect the mountains where legend has persistently placed the lair of the Amazon women. On the border with Bolivia there are the **Parque Nacional da Serra do Divisor** and the **Parque Nacional da Serra da Cutia** in the states of Acre and Rondônia respectively. Closer, but only marginally more accessible by light plane from the state capital Porto Velho, is the **Parque Nacional de Pacaás Novos** in Rondônia that contains examples of both Cerrado and Amazon rainforest. The **Parque Nacional do Araguaia** in the state of Tocantins is in the north part of Bananal, the biggest river island of the world, and borders the Karajá Indian reservation. It is difficult to reach, but it contains what Brazilians crave most: beaches. Although they are riverine rather than marine, it is the closest option for many in the Central Plateau, so the traffic in the park is increasing.

long, one way), at 2263m (7425ft) the highest point of the park on the Teresópolis side; and the track to Pedra do Açu (8km/5 miles long, one way), on the Petrópolis side. All trails are self-guided.

There are two Brazilian parks that are primarily for hiking, combining the spectacle of high mesas and canyons with luxuriant vegetation and the obligatory waterfalls. These are the **Chapada Diamantina** in central Bahia and **Chapada dos Guimarães** in Mato Grosso. Chapada Diamantina features in the Top 10 of Brazilian destinations, combining as it does archaeology (there are 8000-year-old petroglyphs in the Serra das Paridas), one- to five-day treks (within Brazil it is considered the Mecca of trekking) and stunning natural attractions (the Fumaça Waterfall is 380m/1247ft tall). The Chapada dos Guimarães is another Cerrado national park with the added attraction that it is the geodesic centre of South America, which gives it more 'mystical' properties. It is also here where the *friagem* can be experienced. This is one of the oddest meteorological phenomena anywhere on the planet and happens some time in May when the temperature drops suddenly to proclaim the onset of the dry season.

The spectacular coastline of the Brazilian northeast reaches its apotheosis in the undulating sand dunes of the **Parque Nacional dos Lençóis Maranhenses** that rise like hills and where pockets of rainwater form lagoons that act as seasonal refuges for migratory birds. Further down, the **Parque Nacional de Jericoacoara** in Ceará has what is consistently voted the top beach in Brazil and one of the Top 10 in the world. Further south on the same coastal biome, the rocky archipelago of the **Parque Nacional dos Abrolhos** can be reached from the mainland municipalities of Alcobaça or Caravelas in Southern Bahia.

This area also contains northern fragments of Mata Atlântica, the most important of which are in the **Parque Nacional do Monte Pascoal**, **Parque Nacional do Descobrimento** and **Parque Nacional do Pau-Brasil**, the latter of which also contains the last large forest of the now endangered tree that originally baptized the country. The three parks all lie close to each other on the Discovery Coast. As the name suggests, this was the place where Portuguese explorer Pedro Álvares Cabral touched on the

Other Brazilian National Parks

land of Brazil on 22 April 1500, possibly at the mouth of Rio Caí not far from today's Parque Nacional do Descobrimento.

Bahia also contains two extraordinary ecological stations where work is being done for the preservation of two very different endangered species. The Tamar project in the picturesque village of Praia do Forte about one hour north of Bahia's capital, Salvador, is helping to protect breeding colonies of sea turtles, including the rare Leatherback Turtle (*Dermochelys coriacea*). At the other end of the state, south of the city of Ilhéus, the Ecoparque de Una is one of the main protected breeding grounds of that photogenic monkey, the golden lion tamarin, and contains an impressive observation walkway above the rainforest canopy. Both ecological stations can be visited and they make for two very interesting trips.

The Caatinga contains the eroded rocky outcrops and petroglyphs of the remote **Parque Nacional de Sete Cidades** (Seven Cities) in the state of Piauí and, nearer the sea, the caves of the **Parque Nacional de Ubajara** in the state of Ceará. The **Parque Nacional da Serra das Confusões**, not far from the Serra da Capivara, stands on the boundary between Cerrado and Caatinga. In a 2003 decision, UNESCO has strongly 'urged' the Brazilian government to apply to the Serra das Confusões National Park the same management techniques that saved the Serra da Capivara.

The **Parque Nacional do Monte Roraima**, on the frontier with Guyana and Venezuela, is the most difficult-to-get-to of all Amazonian national parks: those who would like to climb the mountain of the same name – an isolated mesa with its own ecosystem that inspired Conan Doyle's *Lost World* – are advised to try from the Venezuelan end. Roraima has two other national parks with no or limited access to the public; the **Parque Nacional da Serra da Mocidade** and the **Parque Nacional Viruá** south of the capital, Boa Vista.

The **Parque Nacional da Amazônia** is the only park in the Amazon basin with a highway running through it: part of the Transamazônica BR-230 cuts across its southern part before São Luiz de Tapajós. This doesn't make it easier to visit, as the nearest city, Santarém, lies 433km (269 miles) to the north. It was

Parque Nacional da Restinga de Jurubatiba

Much further out of Rio the **Parque Nacional da Restinga de Jurubatiba** is the only one protecting a *restinga* ecosystem. It is part of UNESCO's Mata Atlântica Heritage Sites, but its ecosystem is considered far too fragile to allow visitors; unofficially, however, one can drive unhindered to admire the coastal areas of the park.

Climbing the Highest Mountain

It is possible to request permission and obtain clearance to visit (and climb) Brazil's highest mountain, the **Pico da Neblina** in the Parque Nacional do Pico da Neblina on the border with Venezuela, which can be reached from the town of São Gabriel da Cachoeira. This is a park as fascinating as Jaú, made even more interesting by the fact that it is home to one of the most populous native tribes of the Amazon, the Yanomani. With an annual precipitation of 2500mm (98.5 in), it is, however, the wettest part of Brazil, which makes the ascent very difficult; it should only be attempted by skilled mountaineers.

during the construction of this part of the highway, after the national park and the nearby Floresta National de Tapajós had just been created, that the Arara Indians – considered extinct – emerged from the rainforest and beheaded four labourers in 1977. Conflicts with the natives continued for years after that.

In the centre of the east coast, the **Parque Nacional de Caparaó** between the states of Espiritu Santo and Minas Gerais is one with reasonably good infrastructure. Its main claim to fame is that it contains the third highest peak in Brazil, the Pico da Bandeira, which was thought to be the highest in the country until the accidental discovery of the Pico da Neblina in 1946. In Minas Gerais itself, and close to the capital Belo Horizonte, there are the **Parque Nacional da Cerra da Cipó**, over the Espinhaço mountain range, which has provided paleontologists with many valuable fossils and is a very popular park for extreme sports. Not far from there, the **Parque Nacional da Serra da Canastra** is typical of the Cerrado biome, and is the source of the Rio São Francisco which forms the country's third biggest river system. Apart from Amazonian tributaries, the Rio São Francisco is, from its spring to its mouth, the only major wholly Brazilian river.

Two São Francisco tributaries are indirectly responsible for two other national parks on the Minas-Bahia border. The **Parque Nacional Cavernas do Peruaçu** contains more than 140 karst-like caves or grottoes with rock paintings eroded by the Peruaçu River's waters, but is not open for visits as the paintings are still being studied. Only 200km (124 miles) away, the **Parque Nacional Grande Sertão Veredas** is a flat expanse of Cerrado *campo limpo* with riverine wetlands (*veredas*) formed by the Rio Preto and Rio Cariranha; it has recently – and only narrowly – escaped impending transformation to large soya fields.

The south contains several national parks. Not far from the Itaipú dam up the Rio Paraná is the **Parque Nacional de Ilha Grande** (not be confused with the Ilha Grande near Rio de Janeiro) that contains a small archipelago of river islands on the border of the states of Paraná and Mato Grosso do Sul. On the other end of Paraná lies the **Parque Nacional do Superagüi**, a pristine mangrove coastal Mata Atlântica reserve that is easily reached from the capital, Curitiba. Not far away is the **Parque Nacional de Saint-Hilaire/Lange**, almost a continuation of Superagüi below the beauty spot of Ilha do Mel and the busy port of Paranaguá. These three national parks are currently closed to the public.

Further south, there is the **Parque Nacional de São Joaquim** which contains a mixture of Campos and Pinheráis vegetation but without the drama of the canyons of the Aparados da Serra/Serra Geral complex. It is inside the park perimeter on the 1800m (5906ft) high Igreja Hill that, according to legend, the treasure of the Jesuits is buried. It is based on the widely held belief that this Catholic order, who were suddenly expelled from Brazil as they became too powerful, buried all their treasures before they left, expecting to return. They never did.

Parque Nacional da Lagoa do Peixe

The last park right at the border with Uruguay is the **Parque Nacional da Lagoa do Peixe**, a wetland and a sanctuary of birds that has the nickname of the Southern Pantanal. A protected area not on the tourist trail, it is nevertheless worthwhile to visit, especially if continuing on to Uruguay and Argentina.

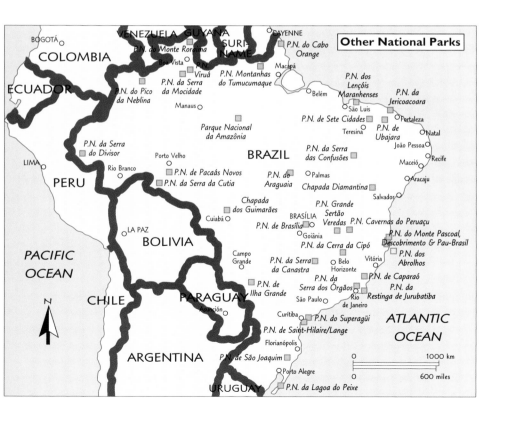

Travel Tips

How to get there

If you are flying to Brazil with TAM or VARIG (which has recently been bought by GOL) you can buy their respective air passes. They are available to anyone purchasing an international ticket into Brazil. They are both priced in US$ and for TAM the current rate ranges between US$560 for four and US$1152 for nine coupons, with children under two years paying only 10% of the adult fare. The VARIG air pass is similarly priced – US$479 for four coupons up to US$1079 for nine. Only one air pass is available per international ticket. Each coupon can be used for one domestic flight (including any connections) that cannot be flown more than once in the same direction. All segments must be booked and confirmed before departure and must be utilized within 21 days of the first air pass flight. Rebooking is permitted at a cost of US$100 per change but rerouting is not.

Car hire

Renting a car in Brazil is also easy and cheap. Almost all rented cars have 'Flex' engines that run on both alcohol and petrol, and alcohol costs about R$1.2–1.5/litre, which is about half the price of petrol. Credit cards are accepted on all stations, however remote. Roads are as good (or as bad) as any in South America, except those near or inside national parks where they are generally bad – a deliberate measure, some people believe, of keeping mass tourism away.

Driving in Brazil

Remember that Brazilians drive on the right and signs are in Portuguese only. If you are renting a car, do so from the airport to avoid driving in the large cities, in particular through São Paulo and Rio de Janeiro. It is not recommended to drive at night in a city or in the country, because illuminations are scant. Pay particular attention to your blind spots since there are many motorcycles and scooters. Similarly, pedestrians tend to cross or walk on motorways, especially in or around the big cities. Lorries tend to indicate right on an open stretch of highway to notify you that you can overtake them. Indicating left means you shouldn't. Note that you can be fined on the spot for many traffic violations, including throwing litter out of your window (even a banana skin in Amazônia). In big cities, you will find unofficial 'street valets' even on a stretch of road where parking is permitted. They will look after your car for a small tip and it is wise to go along with this arrangement.

Passports and visas

Visas for a visit of up to 90 days are not required for the nationals of countries belonging to the EU, except for nationals of Cyprus, Estonia, Latvia, Lithuania, Malta and Romania who do require a visa. Visas are also required for nationals of Andorra, Argentina, Bahamas, Barbados, Bolivia, Chile, Colombia, South Korea, Costa Rica, Croatia, Ecuador, the Philippines, Guatemala, Honduras, Iceland, Israel, Malaysia, Morocco, Monaco, Namibia, Norway, New Zealand, Panama, Paraguay, Peru, Guyana, San Marino, South Africa, Switzerland, Suriname, Thailand, Trinidad and Tobago, Tunisia, Turkey, Uruguay and the Vatican City. Passports have to be valid for at least six months from the date of entry and a return ticket (even if leaving from another Latin American country) may be requested on arrival.

Travel Tips

Independently of visa requirements, visitors to Brazil will be given an immigration coupon which must be kept safe and returned upon leaving the country. Note that US passport holders are also fingerprinted on arrival as a reciprocal measure for the fingerprinting of Brazilian nationals in the USA.

Health precautions

First and foremost, obtain some good and comprehensive travel insurance. Proof of vaccination against polio is compulsory for children aged between three months and six years. Ensure your vaccinations for hepatitis A, typhoid and tetanus are up to date. Medical professionals are not recommending any cholera inoculations any more, insisting instead on proactive behaviour. A yellow fever vaccine is a requirement – sometimes compulsory – for everyone venturing outside of the cities of Rio de Janeiro, São Paulo, Salvador, Recife and Fortaleza, and should be taken at least 10 days before travelling. Proof of vaccination against yellow fever is required for travellers who, in the previous three months before entering Brazil, have

visited or been in transit in Angola, Benin, Bolivia, Burkina Faso, Burundi, Cameroon, Central African Republic, Chad, Colombia, Republic of Congo, Cote d'Ivoire, Democratic Republic of Congo, Ecuador, Equatorial Guinea, Ethiopia, French Guiana, Gabon, Gambia, Ghana, Guinea, Guinea Bissau, Guyana, Kenya, Liberia, Mali, Mauritania, Niger, Nigeria, Panama, Peru, Rwanda, São Tomé and Principe, Senegal, Sierra Leone, Somalia, Sudan, Suriname, Tanzania, Togo, Trinidad and Tobago, Uganda and Venezuela. If you will be travelling in remote areas of the north and the northeast for more than a few days it may be a good idea to take a course of pre-exposure anti-rabies vaccines. If you are bitten by an infected animal (including a vampire bat) you will have up to one week to reach a medical facility for anti-rabies treatment. Where there are mosquitoes, cover yourself at all times. Malarial mosquitoes in the north bite after dark, but those that pass on dengue fever are active during the day. There have been several outbreaks of dengue fever in the south of Brazil during the last two years and the cases

have been increasing in the states of Rio de Janeiro, Pernambuco, São Paulo, and Rio Grande do Norte. Take malaria prophylaxis if travelling to the Amazon or the Pantanal. Tell your health authority where you will be going so that they give you the right medication. Nevertheless, it is best not to be bitten at all, so cover your arms and legs. If you camp in the Pantanal and the Brazilian rainforests you will find that insect repellent is not enough to keep mosquitoes and sand flies off, so take a mosquito net.

If you have an attack of diarrhoea, hydrate yourself. If the diarrhoea persists and/or if the stools are bloody, see a doctor at once.

Do not walk barefoot on the beaches and dunes of northeastern Brazil because of jiggers that might burrow in your feet and deposit their eggs that hatch inside and emerge after a few weeks. Local doctors know how to deal with such problems better than hospitals at home, so you are advised to seek medical help there.

If you have been travelling in the Amazon and the Pantanal and you discover a swelling that becomes larger and starts

Travel Tips

stinging, you may be harbouring a botfly larva. This is a bit more uncomfortable than a jigger, although equally harmless, so you are advised to go promptly to a medical centre. Always drink bottled water, which is easily available. Water from coconuts that are cut in front of you by street vendors is safe. The green, murky *garapa* drink from crushed sugar cane isn't and has been associated with the spread of Chagas disease. Travellers were not thought to be in danger of Chagas disease which is transmitted by bugs found in poor thatched or adobe houses. However, two recent outbreaks in Santa Catarina and Pará were transmitted via the oral route, and involved drinking contaminated wine or sugar cane juice from roadside stands, so do not accept any open drinks from drink vendors.

Electricity

Brazil has a mixture of electricity and pin types on a state and, sometimes, even on a city basis. In general the states of Bahia, Paraná, Rio de Janeiro, São Paulo and Minas Gerais operate at 110/120V, whereas the rest of the country operates at 220/240V. For this reason hotels normally

label their plugs with the voltage and/or mention it clearly in their service manual. If in doubt, check with the hotel reception. The plugs can be either US-style twin flat-blade or Continental European twin-type round pin depending on the establishment. Thankfully, most recent mobile phone and digital camera chargers work with both 110/220V voltages (but check your charger label to be sure). Adapters can be bought locally but are expensive.

Money matters

The currency of Brazil is the *real* R$ (plural *reais*), divided into 100 cents. Current rates are about two to the dollar and four to the pound.

Banking hours

Banking hours in Brazil are normally 10:00–16:00. However, for foreign-exchange transactions 'Casas do cambio' are recommended, since they are open for longer, offer better rates and involve less bureaucracy. (You will need your passport.) You can find such 'cambio' offices in most shopping centres or travel agencies. If you are changing cash, make sure the notes are in mint condition or else they might not be accepted.

Tipping

Brazilians do not normally demand tips, although it is clearly good practice if you want to be looked after or are satisfied with your treatment. Guides (at the end of a tour), room service and bell boys who carry your luggage should be tipped with 2–3 *reais* ('the price of a beer'). Restaurants will automatically include a 10% service which, although voluntary, you are supposed to pay. You do not normally tip barmen if you order drinks directly from the bar. You also don't tip taxi drivers; instead you round upwards any fee on the meter to the nearest *real*. In general, this rounding-up is expected with any transaction paid for in cash.

Telephones

The international code for Brazil is +55, and each city has an area code, such as 011 for São Paolo, 021 for Rio de Janeiro and 061 for Brasília. Within the same area code you need only dial the phone number. So far so good. However, in order to make a phone call from one area code to another within Brazil you also need a carrier code that precedes the access code. For instance, Brasil Telecom's code is 14, so to call a Rio

number through Brasil Telecom you would dial 0+14+21+[phone number]. Embratel's code is 21 so calling the same number through Embratel would involve dialling 0+21+21+[phone number]. This applies to both fixed and mobile numbers. In order to call long distance from Brazil you will again need a carrier. If you use Embratel, say, you would call 00 + 21 + [country code] + [phone number].
If you buy a Brazilian SIM card for use in your mobile phone, you should use the carrier that the mobile company suggests. However, in order to send a text from a Brazilian mobile, you do not dial the operator prefix.
In short, to call a fixed line or a mobile number or send a text to a mobile within the same area code: dial [phone number].
To send a text to a mobile number registered to another area code: dial 0 + [area code] + [phone number].
To call a fixed line or mobile number registered to another area code: dial 0 + [carrier code] + [area code] + [phone number]. To call abroad: dial 0 + [carrier code] + [country code] + [area code] + [phone number].

Behaviour in national parks

Remember that most parks in Brazil are home to endangered species, so do not pick any flowers, seeds, fruits or roots. Do not capture, hunt or maim any animals or disturb their nests.
Do not pick up any furry caterpillars, spiders or centipedes; their hairs can cause a nasty rash.
Rainforest ants are as bad as mosquitoes; some are used by Amazon natives for initiation ceremonies. Do not pick them up, step on them or interfere with their nests.
Respect local communities and their beliefs and customs. Take your litter with you. Never buy merchandise made out of, or including, an animal (skins, feathers, pinned butterflies, insects and so on). Brazil has passed a tough biopiracy law and any attempt to study or export any plants, living organisms (or even soils) requires a special licence. Only swim where locals do. Do not overturn logs, fallen branches or stones as they may harbour snakes or scorpions. For the same reason, if you are camping, check your shoes first thing in the morning, before you step into them.

Further Reading

Carter, David: *Butterflies and Moths* (Dorling Kindersley, 1992). A good accompaniment for Lepidoptera if you are going to the Mata Atlântica.
Gheerbrant, Alain: *The Amazon: Past Present and Future* (Thames and Hudson, 1992). If you read only one book on the Amazon, read this one.
Kricher, John: *A Neotropical Companion* (Princeton University Press, 1999) is the best and immensely readable guide to the flora and fauna of the New World tropics, most of which lie in Brazil.
Malathronas, John: *Brazil: Life, Blood Soul* (Summersdale, 2003). Brazil travelogue from the author of this guide that takes in every biome. The chapters on the Amazon, Bonito and the Pantanal are of special interest.
Spotte, Stephen: *Candiru, Life and Legend of the Bloodsucking Catfishes* (Creative Arts Book Company, 2002). All you need to know about the fish everyone is scared of.
IBAMA produces **Philips guides** in Portuguese for each national park. The last edition of *Brazil: National Parks* (Horizonte Geográfico 2001) translated into English with combined information for all national parks is useful but very much out of date. Once in Brazil, the *Guia Quatro Rodas* published by Editora Abril every year is an excellent buy if you can read rudimentary Portuguese.

Selected Animal and Bird Gallery

Puma

Jaguar

Margay

Ocelot

Jaguarundi

Bush Dog

Crab-eating Fox

Capybara

White-lipped Peccary

Hairy Armadillo

Giant Armadillo

Maned Wolf

Collared Peccary

Ring-tailed Coati

Brazilian Agouti

Lowland Tapir

Giant Anteater

Paca

Grey Short-tailed Opossum

Rock Cavy

Common Opossum

Prehensile-tail Porcupine

Kinkajou

Animals

Red Uakari

Golden-headed Lion Tamarin

Pied Bare-faced Tamarin

Tufted Capuchin

Brown-throated Three-toed Sloth

Vampire Bat

White-bellied Spider Monkey

Marsh Deer

Pampas Deer

Black Howler Monkey

Grey Brocket Deer

Giant Otter

Amazonian Manatee

Pink River Dolphin

Yellow-headed Sideneck Turtle

Red Piranha

Vampire Fish

Spectacled Caiman

Pirarucu

Boa Constrictor

Green Anaconda

Green Iguana

Tegu Lizard

Caiman Lizard

Dyeing Dart Frog

Neuwied's Lancehead

Selected Animal and Bird Gallery

American Kestrel

Crowned Eagle

Harpy Eagle

Snail Kite

Roadside Hawk

Hoatzin

Anhinga

Black Vulture

King Vulture

Turkey Vulture

Crested Caracara

Burrowing Owl

Dusky-legged Guan

Olivaceous Woodcreeper

Red-legged Seriema

Red-winged Tinamou

Black-fronted Piping-Guan

Green Ibis

Scaled Woodcreeper

Buff-Necked Ibis

Birds

Capped Heron

Brazilian Teals

Whistling Heron

Wattled Jacana

Little Blue Heron

Robust Woodpecker

Southern Lapwing

Roseate Spoonbill

Saffron Toucanet

Russet-winged Spadebill

Toco Toucan

Slaty-breasted Wood-rail

Screaming Piha

Brazilian cormorant

Neotropical cormorant

Jabiru Stork

Ringed Kingfisher

Great Kiskadee

Greater Ani

Selected Animal and Bird Gallery

Red-and-Green Macaw

Golden Conure

Plain Parakeet

Scaly-headed Parrot

Vinaceous parrot

Blue-naped Chlorophonia

Versicolored Emerald

Blue-fronted Amazon

Ruby-crowned tanager

Azure Jay

Brazilian Ruby

Tui parakeet

Hyacinth Macaw

Guianan Cock-of-the-rock

Cherry-throated Tanager

Maracanã Macaw

Surucuá Trogon

Green-headed Tanager

Magpie Tanager

Fuscous Flycatcher

Fork-tailed Flycatcher

Birds

Bananaquit

Black Jacobin

White-necked Jacobin

Squirrel Cuckoo

Itatiaia Thistletail

Helmeted Manakin

Noronha Elaenia

Noronha Vireo

Rio de Janeiro Antwren

Purple-throated Euphonia

Sombre Hummingbird

Cattle Egret

Musician Wren

Red-rumped Cacique

Rufous-bellied Thrush

Plain Antvireo

Guira Cuckoo

Grey-hooded Attila

Red-breasted Blackbird

Coal-crested Finch

Check list

Top Mammals
- ☐☐ Amazonian manatee
- ☐☐ Black howler monkey
- ☐☐ Brown capuchin monkey
- ☐☐ Bush dog
- ☐☐ Collared peccary
- ☐☐ Common opossum
- ☐☐ Crab-eating fox
- ☐☐ Giant anteater
- ☐☐ Giant otter
- ☐☐ Golden-headed lion tamarin
- ☐☐ Grey brocket deer
- ☐☐ Grey short-tailed opossum
- ☐☐ Hairy armadillo
- ☐☐ Jaguar
- ☐☐ Jaguarundi
- ☐☐ Kinkajou
- ☐☐ Lesser anteater
- ☐☐ Lowland tapir
- ☐☐ Maned wolf
- ☐☐ Margay
- ☐☐ Marsh deer
- ☐☐ Nine-banded armadillo
- ☐☐ Ocelot
- ☐☐ Paca
- ☐☐ Pampas deer
- ☐☐ Pied bare-faced tamarin
- ☐☐ Pink river dolphin
- ☐☐ Puma, cougar or mountain lion
- ☐☐ Red brocket deer
- ☐☐ Red uacari
- ☐☐ Ring-tailed coati
- ☐☐ Rock cavy
- ☐☐ Six-banded armadillo
- ☐☐ Three-banded armadillo
- ☐☐ Three-toed sloth
- ☐☐ Vampire bat
- ☐☐ White-bellied spider monkey
- ☐☐ White-lipped peccary

Top Rodents
- ☐☐ Agouti
- ☐☐ Brazilian agouti
- ☐☐ Capybara
- ☐☐ Prehensile-tail porcupine

Top Reptiles
- ☐☐ Anaconda
- ☐☐ Boa constrictor
- ☐☐ Caiman lizard
- ☐☐ Dyeing dart frog
- ☐☐ Green iguana
- ☐☐ Neuwied's lancehead
- ☐☐ Spectacled caiman
- ☐☐ Tegu lizard
- ☐☐ Yellow-headed sideneck turtle

Top Fish
- ☐☐ Piracucu
- ☐☐ Red piranha
- ☐☐ Vampire fish

Top Birds
- ☐☐ American Kestrel
- ☐☐ Anhinga (snakebird)
- ☐☐ Azure Jay
- ☐☐ Bananaquit
- ☐☐ Black Jacobin
- ☐☐ Black Skimmer
- ☐☐ Black Vulture
- ☐☐ Black-Beaked Toucan
- ☐☐ Black-capped Antwren
- ☐☐ Black-fronted Piping-Guan
- ☐☐ Black-throated Trogon
- ☐☐ Blue-bellied Parrot
- ☐☐ Blue-fronted Amazon
- ☐☐ Blue-naped Chlorophonia
- ☐☐ Brassy-breasted Tanager
- ☐☐ Brazilian Cormorant
- ☐☐ Brazilian Ruby
- ☐☐ Brazilian Teals
- ☐☐ Buff-Necked Ibis
- ☐☐ Burrowing Owl
- ☐☐ Caatinga (Cactus) Parakeet
- ☐☐ Capped Heron
- ☐☐ Cattle Egret
- ☐☐ Cherry-Throated Tanager
- ☐☐ Chestnut-Bellied Euphonia
- ☐☐ Coal-crested Finch
- ☐☐ Cock-of-the-rock
- ☐☐ Crested Caracara
- ☐☐ Crowned Eagle
- ☐☐ Curl-crested Jay
- ☐☐ Dusky-legged Guan
- ☐☐ Eared Dove
- ☐☐ Festive Coquette
- ☐☐ Fork-Tailed Flycatcher
- ☐☐ Fuscous Flycatcher
- ☐☐ Golden Conure
- ☐☐ Gray-hooded Attila
- ☐☐ Great Kiskadee
- ☐☐ Greater Ani
- ☐☐ Green Ibis

Check list

- ☐☐ Green-Headed Tanager
- ☐☐ Grey-Winged Cotinga
- ☐☐ Guira Cuckoo
- ☐☐ Harpy Eagle
- ☐☐ Helmeted Manakin
- ☐☐ Helmeted Woodpecker
- ☐☐ Hepatic Tanager
- ☐☐ Hoatzin
- ☐☐ Hyacinthe Macaw
- ☐☐ Itatiaia Thistletail
- ☐☐ Jabiru Stork
- ☐☐ King Vulture
- ☐☐ Large-billed Antwren
- ☐☐ Large-Billed Tern
- ☐☐ Large-Tailed Antshrike
- ☐☐ Little Blue Heron
- ☐☐ Long-Billed Woodcreeper
- ☐☐ Magpie Tanager
- ☐☐ Maracanã Macaw
- ☐☐ Masked Tanager
- ☐☐ Musician Wren
- ☐☐ Neotropical Cormorant
- ☐☐ Noronha Elenia
- ☐☐ Noronha Vireo
- ☐☐ Olivaceous Woodcreeper
- ☐☐ Orange-Headed Tanager
- ☐☐ Pale-crested Woodpecker
- ☐☐ Plain Antvireo
- ☐☐ Plain Parakeet

- ☐☐ Plush-crested Jay
- ☐☐ Purple-throated Euphonia
- ☐☐ Red-and-green Macaw
- ☐☐ Red-Bellied Parakeet
- ☐☐ Red-Billed Toucan
- ☐☐ Red-Breasted Blackbirds
- ☐☐ Red-Breasted Toucan
- ☐☐ Red-legged Seriema
- ☐☐ Red-Rumped Cacique
- ☐☐ Red-winged Tinamou
- ☐☐ Ringed Kingfisher
- ☐☐ Rio de Janeiro Antwren
- ☐☐ River Warbler
- ☐☐ Roadside Hawk
- ☐☐ Robust Woodpecker
- ☐☐ Roseate Spoonbill
- ☐☐ Ruby-Crowned Tanager
- ☐☐ Rufous Gnateater
- ☐☐ Rufous-bellied Thrush
- ☐☐ Rufous-capped Motmot
- ☐☐ Rufous-tailed Jacamar
- ☐☐ Russet-winged Spadebill
- ☐☐ Saffron Toucanet
- ☐☐ Scaled Woodcreeper
- ☐☐ Scaly-headed Parrot
- ☐☐ Screaming Piha
- ☐☐ Slaty-breasted Wood-rail

- ☐☐ Smooth-billed Ani
- ☐☐ Snail Kite
- ☐☐ Sombre Hummingbird
- ☐☐ Southern Lapwing
- ☐☐ Squirrel Cuckoo
- ☐☐ Star-Throated Antwren
- ☐☐ Streamer-Tailed Tyrant
- ☐☐ Surucuá Trogon
- ☐☐ Tawny-Browed Owl
- ☐☐ Thrush-Like Wren
- ☐☐ Toco Toucan
- ☐☐ Tufted Antshrike
- ☐☐ Tui Parakeet
- ☐☐ Turkey Vulture
- ☐☐ Turquoise Tanager
- ☐☐ Versicolored Emerald
- ☐☐ Vinaceous parrot
- ☐☐ Violet-capped Woodnymph
- ☐☐ Wattled Jacana
- ☐☐ Whistling Heron
- ☐☐ White-banded Tanager
- ☐☐ White-barred Piculet
- ☐☐ White-Bearded Antshrike
- ☐☐ White-bearded Manakin
- ☐☐ White-Bibbed Antbird
- ☐☐ White-Collared Foliage-gleaner
- ☐☐ White-necked Jacobin
- ☐☐ White-rumped Tanager
- ☐☐ White-Throated Kingbird
- ☐☐ Yellow Tyrannulet
- ☐☐ Yellow-Headed Caracara

Index

Index

Mammals Translated

English name	Brazilian name	Scientific name
Amazonian Manatee	Peixe-boi	*Trichecus inunguis*
Bald Uacari	Uacari	*Cacajao calvus*
Black Howler Monkey	Bugio	*Alouatta caraya*
Brazilian Tapir	Anta	*Tapirus terrestris*
Brown or Tufted Capuchin Monkey	Macaco-prego	*Cebus apella*
Bush Dog	Cachorro-vinagre	*Speothos venaticus*
Collared Peccary	Cateto	*Pecari tajacu*
Common Opossum	Gambá-de-orelha-preta	*Didelphis marsupialis*
Crab-eating Fox	Cachorro-do-Mato	*Cerdocyon hous*
Giant Anteater	Tamanduá bandeira	*Myrmecophaga tridactyla*
Giant Otter	Ariranha	*Pteronura brasiliensis*
Golden-headed Lion Tamarin	Mico-leão-de-cara-dourada	*Leontopithecus chrysomelas*
Grey Brocket Deer	Veado-catingeiro	*Mazama gouazoubira*
Grey Short-tailed Opossum	cuíca	*Monodelphis domestica*
Hairy Armadillo)	Tatú –peludo	*Chaetophractus villosus*
Jaguar	Onça pintada	*Panthera onca*
Jaguarundi	jaguarundi	*Herpailurus yaguarondi*
Kinkajou	kinkajou	*Potos flavus*
Lesser Anteater	Tamanduá-mirim	*Tamandua tetradactyla*
Maned Wolf	Lobo-guará	*Chrysocyon brachyurus*
Margay	Gato-maracajá	*Leopardus wiedii*
Marsh Deer	Cervo-do-pantanal	*Blastocerus dicotomus*
Nine-banded or Giant Armadillo	Tatu-galinha	*Dasypus novemcinctus*
Ocelot	Jaguatirica	*Leopardus pardalis*
Paca	Paca	*Agouti paca*
Pampas Deer	Veado-campeiro	*Ozotoceros bezoarticus*
Pied Bare-faced Tamarin	Sauim-de-coleira	*Saguinus bicolor*
Pink River Dolphin	Boto	*Inia geoffrensis*
Puma	Onça parda	*Puma concolor*
Red Brocket Deer	Veado-mateiro	*Mazama americana*
Rock Cavy	Mocó	*Kerodon rupestris*
Six-banded Armadillo	Tatu-peba	*Euphractus sexcintus*
South American Coati	Quati	*Nasua nasua*
Three-banded Armadillo	Tatú bola	*Tolypeutes tricinctus*
Three-toed Sloth	Bicho-preguiça	*Bradypus variegatus*
Vampire Bat	Morcego-vampiro	*Diaemus youngi*
White-bellied Spider Monkey	Macaco-coatá	*Ateles belzebuth*
White-lipped Peccary	Queixada	*Tayassu peccari*

160

Imprint Page

First edition published in 2008
by New Holland Publishers (UK) Ltd
London • Cape Town • Sydney • Auckland
10 9 8 7 6 5 4 3 2 1
website: www.newhollandpublishers.com

Garfield House, 86 Edgware Road
London W2 2EA
United Kingdom

80 McKenzie Street
Cape Town 8001
South Africa

Unit 1, 66 Gibbes Street
Chatswood, NSW 2067
Australia

218 Lake Road
Northcote, Auckland
New Zealand

Distributed in the USA by
The Globe Pequot Press, Connecticut

Copyright © 2008 in text: John Malathronas
Copyright © 2008 in maps: Globetrotter Travel Maps
Copyright © 2008 in photographs:
Individual photographers as credited (right)
Copyright © 2008 in illustrations:
New Holland Publishers (UK) Ltd
Copyright © 2008 New Holland Publishers (UK) Ltd

All rights reserved. No part of this publication may
be reproduced, stored in a retrieval system or
transmitted, in any form or by any means, electronic,
mechanical, photocopying, recording or otherwise,
without the prior written permission of the publishers
and copyright holders.

ISBN 978 1 84773 135 7

This guidebook has been written by independent
authors and updaters. The information therein represents their impartial opinion, and neither they nor the
publishers accept payment in return for including in the
book or writing more favourable reviews of any of the
establishments. Whilst every effort has been made to
ensure that this guidebook is as accurate and up to date
as possible, please be aware that the facts quoted are
subject to change, particularly the price of food, transport and accommodation. The Publisher accepts no
responsibility or liability for any loss, injury or inconve-
nience incurred by readers or travellers using this guide.

Keep us Current
Information in travel guides is apt to change, which is
why we regularly update our guides. We'd be grateful
to receive feedback if you've noted something we
should include in our updates. If you have new
information, please share it with us by writing to the
Publishing Manager, Globetrotter, at the office nearest
to you (addresses on this page). The most significant
contribution to each new edition will receive a free
copy of the updated guide.

Publishing Manager: Thea Grobbelaar
DTP Cartographic Manager: Genené Hart
Editor: Carla Zietsman

Design and DTP: Nicole Bannister
Cartographer: Carryck Wise
Picture Researchers: Shavonne Govender,
Zainoenisa Manuel
Illustrator: Steven Felmore
Consultants: Marianne Taylor and Terry Roberts

Reproduction by Resolution, Cape Town
Printed and bound in China by C & C Offset Printing
Co., Ltd.

Dedication:
To my mother, who first travelled to Brazil and wisely
urged me to visit the country.

Acknowledgments:
There are many people the author wishes to thank for
their help during the compilation of this book, but the
following deserve particular mention: Tom Falcão and
Glauco Fuzinatto from the Brazilian Embassy in the
UK; Fuad Atala from the Rio Tourism Authority;
David Maziteli from FSB Comunicações and Anna
Halley, at WHD Comunicação, Brasília; Leo
Nascimento and Marcos Sá Corrêa in Itatiaia; Izar
Araújo Aximoff from the Botanical Gardens in Rio de
Janeiro; Alexandre Justino in Tijuca; Gibby Zobel in
London; Luiz Carlos Oliveira all over Goiás; Renato
Gusmão at the Parque das Emas; Cristiano Santa in the
Chapada dos Veadeiros; Amazonas Índio Turismo in
Manaus; Camelot Inn in Alto Paraíso de Goiás;
Pousada Cristal da Terra in São Jorge; Gil's Tours in
the Pantanal.

Photographic credits:
Heather Angel/Natural Visions: pages 6 (centre),
10, 33, 38 (centre), 56 (bottom), 72, 78 (bottom), 86, 91,
140 (top); **Otto Bathurst/jonarnoldimages.com:**
half title page, page 140 (centre); **Jeff Collett/Natural
Visions:** page 56 (top); **Richard Coomber/Natural
Visions:** pages 22 (centre), 78 (top), 94 (top and
bottom), 128 (centre), 139; **Gerald Cubitt:** back
cover (centre), pages 18, 66 (centre), 105, 135, 140
(bottom); **Richard Day/Natural Visions:** page 117;
Gregory Guida/Natural Visions: page 55; **John
Malathronas:** pages 26, 38 (top and bottom), 40, 44,
52, 59, 78 (centre), 100, 108 (centre), 114, 119, 130;
Buddy Mays: title page, contents page, back cover
(top), pages 15, 21; **Candy McManiman/http://
webserv.nhl.nl/~ribot/english:** page 29; **Nature
Picture Library/Photo Access:** pages 6 (top), 22
(top and bottom), 37, 47, 48, 66 (top and bottom), 75,
92, 108 (top and bottom), 125, 127, 128 (top and bottom), 132; **Oxford Scientific/Photo Access:** page
65; **Pete Oxford/naturepl.com/Photo Access:**
front cover, contents page; **Pictures Colour
Library:** back cover (bottom) page 123; **Brian
Rogers/Natural Visions:** pages 29, 84, 94 (centre);
Francesca Tomasinelli/Natural Visions: page 7
(bottom); **Michael Windle/Natural Visions:** page
56 (centre).

Cover: Ocelot (front); giant blue morpho butterfly, young
Coati, Tri-Colour and Red Rainbow fish (back, top to bottom).
Half title page: A blue Poison Arrow Frog.
Title page: Oxbow bend on the Amazon River in
northwest Brazil.
Contents page: A Caiman basking with a butterfly on
his snout.